D0904143

Hibernia

Literature and Nation in Victorian Ireland

A series of facsimile reprints chosen and introduced by
JOHN KELLY

James Fintan Lalor

Collected
Writings
1918

Woodstock Books
Poole · Washington D.C.
1997

This edition first published 1997 by
Woodstock Books
c/o Cassell plc, 3 Fleets Lane
Poole, England BH15 3AJ
and
Cassell Academic
P.O. Box 605, Herndon
VA. 20172

ISBN 1 85477 219 8
Original edition of 1918 edited by
L. Fogarty, preface by Arthur Griffith,
published by Talbot Press, Dublin.
New matter copyright © John Kelly 1997

British Library Cataloguing-in-Publication Data
A catalogue record for this book is
available from the British Library

Library of Congress Cataloging-in-Publication Data
Lalor, James Fintan, d. 1849.
    Collected writings / James Fintan Lalor.
       p. cm. – (Hibernia)
    Includes bibliographical references (p.   )
    ISBN 1-85477-219-8 (alk. paper)
       1. Ireland – Politics and government – 19th century – Sources.
    I. Title.   II. Series.
    DA950.23.L35A2 1997
    320.9415 – dc20   96-35549
                                                                    CIP

Printed and bound in Great Britain by
Smith Settle
Otley, West Yorkshire LS21 3JP

Introduction

'I could not be persuaded that I had before me, in the poor, distorted, ill-favoured hunch-backed little creature, the bold propounder of the singular doctrines in the *Nation* letters.' So the Young Irelander Michael Doherty wrote to Charles Gavan Duffy on first meeting James Fintan Lalor, and Lalor has remained as much an enigma to later generations as he was to his contemporaries. Facts about his short and infirm life are not easy to ascertain, and it was not until nearly fifty years after his death that any of his writings were generally available. Yet he was recalled as a powerful radical commentator on the Irish constitution and economy, and after his work was published in book form from 1895 he was hailed and annexed by distinct Irish groups as variously a nationalist, a socialist, and an agrarian reformer. By 1918 three separate editions of his writings had appeared, the best of which was the present one, edited by Lilian Fogarty and prefaced with a substantial biographical introduction which still holds much interest. However, written in the politically charged days of 1918, and relying upon oral testimony gathered nearly seventy years after Lalor's death, her account requires both amplification and modification, especially given the distinguished subsequent research by Thomas O'Neill and David Buckley.

Born in March 1807 at Tinakill, Abbeyliex, in what is now Co. Laois, Lalor was the eldest of twelve children, but a disease of the spine, attributed by some to a congenital condition and by others to a nurse dropping him in infancy, left him a hunchback and in chronic bad health for the rest of his life. While his father's comfortable financial situation was able to shield him from the adverse material effects his disabilities might otherwise have caused, the psychological effects were more pervasive. Although not nearly so Romantic and reclusive as Miss Fogarty suggests, nor so removed from the realities of political life as Duffy was later to pretend in *Four Years*, Lalor nevertheless found his scope for public action curtailed by his physical condition, and his passionate mind was forced to brood over certain ideas until they became unquestioned and unshakeable convictions. This gives his prose energy and a driving intensity, but it also led him to exaggerate the inevitability of his conclusions and underestimate the objections to them.

His father, Patrick ('Honest Pat') Lalor, was a well-to-do farmer, one of the 'middlemen' of whom William Carleton disapproved, who prospered between the head landlord and the poorer tenants, and by 1832 he was leasing nearly 1000 acres on two farms. Lalor, who apparently helped in administering his properties, described him as belonging 'to the highest class of what in this country are called "Gentlemen-farmers" '. This economic and social position was to colour the younger Lalor's thinking; he was not, as Lilian Fogarty suggests, a peasant speaking for the peasants, and, although he himself claimed that his station in society put him 'at the *point of contact* where all ranks of Repealers touch', his central concern in all his writings is the Irish tenant farmer; he has little to say about agricultural (or 'common' as he described them) labourers.

Pat Lalor did not send his son to local schools, but had him educated – somewhat patchily it seems – at home until the age of seventeen, when Fintan was enrolled at Carlow College, one of the most prestigious of Irish Catholic schools. There his studies were frequently interrupted by recurrent ill-health which forced him to return home after only one year, but it may have been at Carlow that he first came across the eighteenth-century theories of natural law and social contract that were to shape his later theories. His lack of formal education was later remarked, and Miss Fogarty's fanciful account of his immersion in the classics and contemporary French authors seems plainly contradicted by his own admission that he had all his life 'suffered from a dearth of books'. But what little he read he read to purpose, and made part of his intense meditation on the state of Irish society.

Little is known of his activities after his arrival home from school in February 1826. There is evidence that he was apprenticed for a short period to Dr Jacob, a local doctor, but none at all that he visited France (as Lilian Fogarty asserts).

No letters or documents mention such an expedition, and his always precarious health makes it unlikely that he ever risked a journey abroad. He was certainly at home in 1831 when his father's political career took a vigorous turn. Pat Lalor had long been a staunch follower of O'Connell, and as a prosperous member of the community his support was welcomed. He backed the campaign for Catholic Emancipation, and, when this was won, threw himself into the new agitation to repeal the Act of Union. But he was particularly prominent in the so-called Tithe War, the campaign to abolish the contributions that Catholics and Nonconformists were obliged to render to the Church of Ireland. He proclaimed publicly that he would pay no more tithes, and when twenty-five of his sheep were distrained in consequence, he marked them with the word 'TITHE' so that no-one would buy them. (The wretched creatures finally expired while being transported across Yorkshire.) These activities drew the attention of the authorities, and in 1832 he was invited to give evidence before a House of Lords Committee on Tithes. There he defended his action as passive resistance to an unjust system, and advocated 'the non-dealing system' (an early form of what was later called 'boycotting') through which anyone buying goods that had been distrained would be shunned. In the light of his son's later insistence on the legal basis of political action, it is significant that Pat Lalor defended his action as being entirely within the law, since 'the best legal advice' had assured him that he could not be compelled to pay tithes and that he could legitimately withhold them as long as he complied with the law by surrendering distrained goods.

In the same year as he appeared before the Tithe Committee, Pat Lalor took advantage of the newly won Catholic Emancipation by standing for Parliament against a local landlord, Sir Charles Coote. Party feeling ran high; a bitter and keenly fought campaign left three people dead, and Lalor returned at the head of the poll. He served at Westminster from 1832 to 1835, where, it seems, the fashionable world would have raised a quizzical eyebrow at his son's description of him as a gentleman farmer, since one young Liberal noted condescendingly that 'Lalor shews that he has never been in gentleman's society before. I believe it was only last year that Sir Henry Parnell ... presented him with a coat, being the first he had ever been the owner of, to appear in.' Although Fintan Lalor does not seem to have played any active part in his father's campaigns, the controversies of these days alerted him to the fact and possibilities of political agitation, and in his article in the fourth number of the *Irish Felon* in 1848 he counted 'the present contest' as having begun 'eighteen years' before (see p. 105). Not that his politics were to resemble his father's, for he soon took a violent aversion to Repeal politics in general and Daniel O'Connell in particular. Although there may have been a element of oedipal rejection in this position, it was initially given a theoretical basis through his friendship in the 1830s with the agrarian radical William Conner.

II

In her Biographical Introduction, Lilian Fogarty suggests that Lalor derived his ideas on land tenure from a supposed co-operative system current among the ancient Gaels. The idea that the ancient Gaels held land in common rests on a misconception, but was very fashionable at the time she was writing. There is, however, no evidence that Lalor had any knowledge of agricultural practices among the ancient Irish. Miss Fogarty's further contention that (apart from Tone and Davis) 'no other writers moulded Lalor's thought on nationality and economic questions', is also incorrect, and Lalor himself provides clues to the real sources of his ideas when he invokes the eighteenth-century English jurist Sir William Blackstone, and the seventeenth-century empiricist philosopher John Locke (p. 101). Their influence is felt in his later work; his first introduction to agrarian politics came through the eccentric Irish landowner William Conner.

Conner, the illegitimate son of General Arthur Condorcet O'Connor, and a cousin of Fergus O'Connor the Chartist leader, was a wealthy landlord who dedicated considerable sums to the cause of tenant rights. He inaugurated his campaign on behalf of the peasants in 1832 at a public meeting which Lalor almost certainly attended, since it took place at Inch, not far from his home. In his speech there, Conner insisted that all agitation for Irish political independence was pointless unless preceded by sweeping land reforms. He attacked the landlords for refusing to reduce rents set during the inflationary days of the Napoleonic Wars, and argued that, since the supply of land was fixed, the landlords were in effect monopolists, and should be subject to the same legal restraints as other monopolists. This would inevitably entail State intervention in Irish agrarian affairs, and Conner urged that a public tribunal should monitor the relations between landlords and tenants, and secure the latter against arbitrary eviction.

When he issued this speech as a pamphlet in 1835 he added a preface, greatly amplifying his ideas on state regulation. He maintained that the rights of tenants could only be protected 'by the State's abridging the landlords' power over the land' and urged that the State should guarantee security of tenure by extending English tenant rights to Ireland and by forbidding eviction for anything but non-payment of rent. Through the 1830s and 1840s Conner published a stream of further pamphlets and spoke at innumerable public meetings, pressing his views with such vigour that, following a speech at Mountmellick in 1842, he was tried for sedition and sentenced to six months imprisonment. Soon after this he was ousted from O'Connell's Repeal Association for advocating a rent-strike by the tenant farmers. The expulsion confirmed his suspicion of merely political agitation, and in a pamphlet of 1846 he denounced not only O'Connell's legalistic duplicities but also the 'nonsensical, bombastical and perfidious *Nation*'.

III

By this time he and Lalor had parted company, and their disagreements were to have a vehement public airing at the Holycross fiasco in 1847 (see pp. 47-51). Commentators have subsequently disputed the extent and length of Conner's influence on Lalor, but it certainly seems to have been strong as late as the summer of 1843, when – in the 'Year of Repeal' and 'Monster Meetings'– Lalor wrote at least two letters to the Conservative Prime Minister Sir Robert Peel, offering to help suppress Repeal agitation in return for State regulation of land holdings. Writing, significantly, not from his home address, but from 'Miss Butler's, Maryborough', and marking his letter 'private', he told Peel that he had 'long seen and felt … the absolute necessity which exists, that *all* agitation for political objects should entirely cease, before any improvement can be effected in the condition of the Irish people', that he was 'most anxious that the present Repeal-movement should be speedily and safely suppressed … fully and for ever', and that to 'effect that object I wish to contribute whatever little aid it may be in my power to give.'

He went on to impress upon Peel that this 'little aid' was in fact quite unique: 'I cannot help considering that *I* am … better acquainted with the existing movement … than most, perhaps than any one … I can scarcely conceive … that any person holding an official situation can possibly know the agitation and agitators so thoroughly and truly as I do.' He explained that his father 'was, and I regret to say, still continues, a zealous and active Repealer', and that he had himself once been 'something *more* than a mere Repealer, but that 'Mr. O'Connell, his *agitators*, and his series of wretched agitations, first *disgusted* me into a conservative in point of *feeling*, and reflection and experience have *convinced* me into one in point of *principle*. I have been *driven* into the conviction, more strongly confirmed by everyday's experience, that it is only to a Conservative Government, to her landed proprietors, and to peace that this country can look for any improvement in her social condition.' Indeed, he thought it 'probable that I shall soon be *obliged* to join the Conservative party openly and actively'.

Peel took this seriously enough to pass the letter on to the Home Secretary, Sir James Graham, and to Albert, the Prince Consort, and he encouraged Lalor to submit detailed proposals. This he evidently did, for although his second letter cannot be traced, Graham's notes on it reveal that it comprised at least 50 numbered proposals, and extended over at least 48 pages. Peel also asked the Earl De Grey, Lord Lieutenant of Ireland, for a biographical account of his intriguing correspondent, and was informed that Lalor had 'no ostensible means of his own. He acts as an overseer to his father's farming affairs, and I do not hear a favourable account of his character or disposition. He is said to be not deficient in intelligence, but his education is of a very low stamp. The Father is a very intelligent but unscrupulous man. He endeavoured to sell his property in order to emigrate, but without success, very much to the regret of the other gentry.' Even without this report, Lalor's ideas would have been too radical for a Tory administration to contemplate, and Peel does not appear to have followed them up.

In the light of Lalor's *Felon* letters this correspondence with Peel seems extraordinary: his declaration of Conservative principles, his willingness to act as a government agent to subvert Repeal, his faith in the landlords, and in government intervention – all these would have complicated Griffith's and Fogarty's views of him, and point to the lingering influence of Conner. Yet a measure of consistency between his earlier and later positions is found in the very urgency and exaggerated self-confidence of his utterances. They register the desperate insistence of a man who has grasped the solution that all others have missed, a man who has a mission and who is in a unique position to *know* that he is right. This is the key which reconciles the apparently divergent opinions in this letter to his later views: Conservatives or Confederates, he will associate with any party willing to adopt the policies that, he is convinced, can alone save Ireland. In 1843 the best chance seemed to lie with Peel and the landlords; by 1848 the experience of the Famine has disabused him of any hope in landlords or state intervention, and he had turned to other allies.

As the letter to Peel reveals, his policies were now totally opposed to those of his father. Despite Lilian Fogarty's claim that he had grown tired of the political veniality of O'Connell and his followers, Pat Lalor (who in 1835 had stood unsuccessfully for re-election to Parliament) was still on his son's admission 'a zealous and active Repealer', and what must have been years of friction between father and son culminated in 1845, when Fintan was ordered to quit the house. He struck out for himself in Dublin, where, still reliant on an allowance from his father, his health soon broke down. Courageously, he refused appeals to return to Tinakill, and, when his condition improved, joined a banking venture set up to make loans available to the poor. He visited Belfast to enquire into a similar institution there, and evidently liked the city, for in September 1845 he applied – unsuccessfully – for a post as librarian and teacher at the Belfast Mechanics Institute. Back in Dublin, he fell so severely ill during the winter that he thought he was dying, and in March 1846 he was brought home. He did not die, but his recovery was long and uncertain.

IV

Towards the end of his recuperation, in the late autumn of 1846, Lalor determined to make another attempt to get his ideas on Irish agriculture more widely accepted. As is abundantly clear from all his published writing, it was the calamity of the Famine that now spurred him into action. From its first year he seemed to have grasped that it was a national catastrophe on an unprecedented scale, but he was convinced that if only his ideas were implemented its effects would be quickly alleviated. This desperate certainty made him all the more urgent for the adoption of his policies. He had been unsuccessful with Peel and the Conservatives, who were now in any case out of office, and he could have no truck with the despised O'Connell, nor with his potential allies, the English Whigs. But O'Connell had broken with the Young Irelanders, the intellectual and radical wing of his movement, who had marched out of his headquarters in Conciliation Hall in July 1846 and were in process of setting up a new organization, the Irish Confederation. Lalor later detected the hand of Providence in all this, recalling in a *Felon* letter that he had been 'biding my time when the potato failure hurried a crisis' and that in this crisis the secession of the Young Irelanders from the Repeal

Association seemed 'specially pre-ordained and produced in order to aid me'. At the time he was somewhat less convinced that all was predestined; indeed, two recent articles in the *Nation* gave him concern that the Young Irelanders might be going down the wrong road by trying to appease the landlords. Since the inaugural meeting of the Confederation, advertised for 13 January 1847, was only a few days away, he dashed off a letter begging Duffy not to pass any resolutions that would prevent his co-operating with the new association.

This letter, although it was never published in the newspaper, forms the first in the series that Lalor contributed to the *Nation* during the late spring of 1847, and it records a shift in his thought since the letter to Peel. The influence of William Conner persists in his conviction that the land question is of infinitely greater importance than Repeal, and his later advocacy of a rent strike may also have owed something to Conner (although his father's passive resistance during the Tithe War would also have acted as a model here). Where Lalor now differed from Conner was over landlords' rights and state intervention. Conner wanted to reform, not abolish, the landlords: as became evident in pamphlets and letters he wrote in the mid-forties, he feared that their abuse of what he considered their monopolistic powers would lead to a violent reaction, culminating in revolution and their ruin. Since they themselves were too narrowly self-interested to see this, it was imperative that the government should intervene and impose a just system of land tenure, so that society should not be shattered. But the Famine had convinced Lalor that Westminster had neither the power nor the desire to come to the aid of Irish farmers, and he was soon to write off the landlords as robbers and aliens.

V

These new views on landlords' rights were shaped by his excursions into Blackstone's *Commentaries on the Laws of England* (1765-9), and Locke's *Two Treatises of Government* (1690), and the influence of these two works informs Lalor's letters to both the *Nation* and the *Felon*. Although he declared himself 'no lawyer thank God', and denounced the legal juggling of O'Connell and his followers, he found the beginning of the second book of *Commentaries* of great interest (he cites in particular 'the first chapter of Blackstone second book'). Here Blackstone discusses the legal questions raised by colonization and the rights attached to land ownership. While he condones the settlement of empty or sparsely-inhabited countries, he is censorious of conquest which involves the exploitation and massacre of indigenous peoples, intimating that such behaviour is contrary to nature, reason, and Christianity. Lalor took this to be a condemnation of colonial conquest as contravening natural and divine law, and interpreted it as thus invalidating the conquest of Ireland and the subsequent appropriation and possession of the land by the invaders.

To define the extent of this possession, Lalor once again consulted Blackstone's second book. Blackstone explained that 'Land hath also in its legal signification, an indefinite extent, upwards as well as downwards. *Cujus est solum, ejus est usque ad coelum* is the maxim of the law, upwards; therefore no man may erect any building, or the like, to overhang another's land … So that the word "land" includes not only the face of the earth, but everything under it, or over it.' Lalor (whose emphasis on 'soil' when discussing the land question derives from this source) construed this as applying not merely to individual desmenes or plots of land, but to the whole territory of Ireland, maintaining that 'the entire ownership of Ireland, moral and material, up to the sun, and down to the centre, is vested of right in the people of Ireland; that they and none but they are the land-owners and law-makers of this island; that all laws are null and void not made by them; and all titles to land invalid not conferred and confirmed by them; and that this full right of ownership may and ought to be asserted and enforced by any and all means which God has put in the power of man. In other, if not plainer words, I hold and maintain that the entire soil of a country belongs of right to the people of that country, and is the rightful property not of any one class, but of the nation at large' (p. 60). He went on to argue that, this being the case, each holder of land held it in trust from the people of Ireland and must therefore 'bear full, true, and undivided fealty, and allegiance to the nation, and the laws of the nation whose lands he holds'. This, being a natural and divine law, transcends all other 'constitutions, and charters and articles, and franchises', and is of particular significance in the present crisis since the conduct of the landlords in the Famine indicated to Lalor that most of them were traitors to Ireland. Whereas in England the land and property of treasonable subjects reverted to the Crown, in Ireland, he maintained, it returned to the people.

Using these interpretations, Lalor moved the debate about land from legalistic squabbles over individual deeds and contracts to the larger arena of natural law and inalienable rights. In doing this he called not merely on the aid of Blackstone, but also on Locke's two treatises on government. Locke argued that mankind had amended its original state of nature by forming societies based on a social contract whereby leaders were entrusted with the power of rule in order to protect property, rights, and lives as they existed under natural law. This contract depended upon the consent of the people, and if a leader tried to exercise tyrannical power he could be legally overthrown by his subjects. Lalor argued that the conquest of Ireland had not been by consent but was an undesired usurpation subsequently maintained by tyranny. The upheaval caused by the Famine (a consequence, he insisted, of that very tyranny) gave Ireland not only the right but also the opportunity to establish a new social contract. Freely interpreting Locke's second treatise, he wrote that when 'independent families have united into separate tribes, and tribes swelled into nations ... each tribe or nation has but either one or other of two available rights to stand upon – they must take and maintain territorial possession by consent and agreement with all other tribes and nations; or they must take and hold by the *tenure of chivalry*, in the right of their might'. As his disgust with the Ascendancy grew, he informed John Mitchel that his object was 'to repeal the Conquest – not any part or portion but the whole and entire conquest of seven hundred years', and that 'the absolute (allodial) ownership of the lands of Ireland is vested, of right in the people of Ireland – that they, and none but they, are the first landowners and lords paramount as well as the lawmakers of this island – that all titles to land are invalid not conferred or confirmed by them'.

VI

These arguments sound throughout the letters Lalor contributed to the *Nation* and the *Felon*. Duffy had been impressed by the force and intensity of his first letter, and he invited him to write publicly for the *Nation*. Thereupon, as he later recalled, Lalor 'wrote three letters in quick succession, which were marvels of passionate persuasive rhetoric'. On 25 January 1847, before these were published, Lalor also wrote privately to the leading members of the Confederation, setting out his ideas at some length, and, although this communication was not published until it appeared in the *Felon* seventeen months later, it may be considered a part of the *Nation* series.

The letters in this series amplify the lessons he had learned from Locke and Blackstone, and have four interlinked themes: the greater importance of the Land question over Repeal; the fact and consequences of the Famine; the role to be played in Irish politics and agriculture by the landlords; and the importance of preserving Irish peasant proprietors and transforming them into a sturdy yeomanry.

Afraid that the seceders might fall back into the trap of Repeal despite their break with O'Connell, his first letter exhorted Duffy to replace the policy of Repeal with a more general aim of 'independence', and he denounced Repeal as a 'leaky collier-smack, with a craven crew to man her and a sworn dastard and forsworn traitor at the helm'. The land is a 'mightier question … one beside which Repeal dwarfs down into a petty parish question'. Such sentiments lay behind his petition to Peel, but now he goes further and explains why the land question is so important. In the first place, it is not, at the philosophical level, merely a question of political adjustment but, more profoundly, concerns 'that greatest of all our rights on this side of heaven – God's grant to Adam and his poor children for ever'. In the second place, and at a more practical level, he argues that the land question will engage the hearts and minds of the people of Ireland in a far deeper and more energetic way than Repeal can. Repeal is an 'impracticable absurdity', based on obscure legal niceties, without moral and physical force to back it up, and for which the Irish peasant will never be induced to fight. Nor can it hope to make inroads on entrenched English positions. But by transferring the struggle to the land the Irish would be fighting a defensive war that would oblige the English forces to break ranks, and expose themselves. Moreover, the Irish case would be based on the secure principle of natural law that no one has authority over another without consent, and that any attempt to exercise enforced rule may be lawfully resisted. Lalor went on to expand this into the more general Lockean principle 'that every distinct community or nation of men is owner of itself; and can never of right be bound to submit to be governed by another people'.

He advocates what he calls '*moral insurrection*' as a way of asserting such rights; by this he meant the peaceful appropriation and exercise of the powers of government. He realises that this will provoke an English military response, so that moral insurrection is useless without physical force to defend it. Repeal cannot deliver this force, but the cause of independence, if – and only if – tied to the redistribution of land, would galvanize the Irish peasants into defensive military action. The crying need is for a genuinely national movement to organize and direct this action, and the need is urgent since the Famine is destroying the small tenant farmers, and with those farmers Ireland herself, for they are 'the sole strength and hope of this island'. The Confederates have it in their power to forge and lead that new and essential national movement, if only they will link the cause of independence to that of the land.

There was another possible source of leadership, and one in which the Confederates under the leadership of the landlord William Smith O'Brien placed great hopes: a national and pro-Repeal aristocracy. In 1843 Lalor himself had told Peel that Ireland depended on 'her landed proprietors ... for any improvement in her social condition', but he now thought any trust in them was forlorn. Nevertheless, since it was dear to the heart of Duffy and the *Nation*, he agreed to try to rouse the gentry. The recent formation of an 'Irish Party' by the landlords gave him some grounds for encouragement, although he suspected that this would turn out to be less a national organization than a narrow landlord pressure group. His letters to the *Nation* are largely addressed to the landlords, and urge them to throw in their lot with the people. In these letters (which Duffy apparently censored), Lalor combines arguments based on Blackstone and Locke with a rhetoric taken from another of his preferred writers, Thomas Carlyle. In the recently published *Past and Present* Carlyle had appealed to the English gentry to reassume their responsibilities as leaders of a nation in crisis. Lalor now tries something similar with the Irish aristocracy, but to describe his letters as appeals would be to falsify their tone and intention: they are more in the nature of an ultimatum, spelling out the terms on which history and the Irish people will allow this hitherto 'alien class' a place in the new order of society.

Of the fact that the new order must come, indeed is coming, Lalor has no doubt. The Famine is a catastrophe, but the Famine is also an opportunity. It 'is one of those events which come now and then to do the work of ages in a day, and change the very nature of an entire nation at once'. It has shown how rotten a social contract such as the Irish, based on conquest instead of consent, must be: 'it is time to see it is God's will that society should stand dissolved, and assume another shape and action; and he works his will by human hands and natural agencies'. What is required is not a new *political* arrangement but a new *social* constitution, and, in words he will repeat a year later, he instructs his readers that 'Political rights are but paper and parchment. It is the social constitution that determines the condition and character of people, that makes and moulds the life of man.'

It is incumbent upon the landlords, since they claim to be owners of the soil, and are at least in part responsible for the present catastrophe, to help the people. In fact, if they want to survive, they have no choice: they need the people more than the people need them, for their power is gone, stripped away not by violence but 'by the visitation of God in the order of nature. A clear original right returns and reverts to the people - the right of establishing and entering into a new social arrangement.' The inauguration of the landlords' 'Irish Party' seems a step in the right direction, so long as it does not become merely a landowners' club, and in his letter of 25 May 1847 Lalor sets out an elaborate blueprint for a genuinely 'National Council' made up of separate but articulated associations of landlords, tenants and tradesmen. Above all, the landlords must end their dependence on England and declare their allegiance to their own country. Lalor does not insist that they must become Repealers: he does not require a political undertaking, which would mean little, but a social and economic commitment that would mean a great deal, the commitment to protect the small farmers of Ireland and not to assist the Famine in converting them into landless labourers.

And this was the real horror of the Famine for Lalor: it threatened to annihilate the small tenant farmer. With Irish agricultural labourers he had little concern, and with the urban working class even less. (So his adoption into the pantheon of Irish socialists is, to say the least, dubious.) His hopes, and the foundation of his economic theory, lay with the tenant farmers, including the half a million families who subsisted on farms of less than ten acres. It was crucial to Lalor's plans that this class should not only survive but be strengthened since he believed that a 'secure and independent agricultural peasantry is the only base on which a people ever rises, or ever can be raised; or on which a nation can safely rest.' He did not suppose that a strong yeomanry was the only requirement for Ireland's future. His definition of 'all that Ireland wants' envisages a mixed economy: 'equal liberty, and equal laws, science and art, manufacture and trade, respect and renown; wealth to the merchant, security and comfort to the cottage; its pride of power and place to the castle, fame and fortune to genius and talent; all of that which ennobles and endears to man the land he lives in'. Here 'security and comfort to the cottage' takes its place as but one element in a healthy body politic, but in fact Lalor thought it the indispensable and immutable condition of economic health: 'It is an abundant agriculture alone that creates and sustains manufacturers and arts, and traffic', since food is essential to all classes and trades. This, he insists, has been true of all societies at all times; it is the 'ordinance of God and law of Nature'.

VII

And yet Irish agriculture as he conceives it is being destroyed before his eyes. The failure of the potato has brought hardship, but need not, he argues, bring utter destitution if only the people are allowed to retain their rents, their land, and their seed-corn. But this is what the landlords and the English government will not permit. Their inept economic policies and selfishness are destroying any hope of saving the poorer peasants, and as the Famine hit harder, Lalor advocated a rent-strike. The Young Irelanders balked at this: while he was welcomed to the Council of the Confederation, the organization would not adopt his policies, although those policies were to influence Mitchel and Devin Reilly, in particular, and in time were to help split the Confederation's ranks. The arguments against Lalor were recalled by Duffy in *Four Years:* 'To me Lalor's theory seemed a fantastic dream. His angry peasants, chaffing like chained tigers, were creatures of the imagination – not living people through whom we had to act'. Duffy pointed out that the Famine had made the people apathetic and servile rather than warlike, and that in this situation not only could a peasant uprising not succeed, but would alienate the Confederation from 'the classes upon whom we relied for ultimate success' (by which he meant the gentry and middle classes who were sympathetic to Repeal). Smith O'Brien, himself a considerable landlord, assured Duffy that the Irish gentry were coming round to Repeal and implored him to 'abstain from attacking the landlords as a class'. In these circumstances Duffy used all his influence to persuade Mitchel to abide by the agreed Confederate policies.

But as the Confederation tried to work out its political and economic policies, the fissures within it became more apparent. In March 1847 it delegated Smith O'Brien to formulate an agreed manifesto, but his pamphlet *Reproductive Employment* pleased no one and both Mitchel and Duffy provided alternative documents. Duffy urged that the Confederation should infiltrate as many constitutional institutions as possible, while Mitchel, already coming under Lalor's influence, proposed a strike against the poor rate. Although Mitchel was later to tell Lalor that he had accepted his ideas by the summer of 1847 (see pp. 120-3) he would not yet come out for them publicly, although he recommended Lalor privately to O'Brien (see pp. 125-7).

Lalor knew nothing of this, and, disappointed with the Confederate response to his policies, and increasingly convinced that its strategy of conciliating the landlords was futile, he decided upon direct action. In September 1847 he organized a meeting of tenants at Holycross, Co. Tipperary in an attempt to establish a Tenants' Association. Here Lalor ran foul of local agitators, who thought he was poaching on their preserves, and of William Conner, who travelled down from Dublin apparently with the main intention of abusing him. The account of the proceedings given below (pp. 47-51), is taken from the sympathetic *Nation*, and is restrained. Less friendly papers made merry over the collapse of the platform and told how the audience, after voting for the Association with a show of hands, carried Lalor off to a local pub as Conner harangued the emptying hall.

Nothing came of the meeting, and the farcical proceedings dulled Lalor's appetite for public agitation. Nevertheless, the deteriorating state of the country, the deaths and privations of its people as the Famine bit harder, drove him into a more extreme militant rhetoric, but this did not find an outlet until the *Felon* was established in 1848. Although Mitchel finally left the Confederation in early 1848, and wrote to assure Lalor of his support shortly afterwards,

Lalor never contributed to Mitchel's *United Irishman*, perhaps out of pique for the earlier rejection of his rent-strike plan. Meanwhile the French Revolution of February 1848 fed Lalor's (and many other Irishmen's) dreams of a successful revolution at home. Mitchel's arrest on charges of treason-felony changed Lalor's attitude towards him. Now hailing Mitchel as the Irish champion, he agreed to contribute to the *Irish Felon*, the newspaper set up by Mitchel's brother-in-law, John Martin, to succeed the banned *United Irishman*.

VIII

Convinced that the country was ripe for armed revolt, and alarmed by the Government's suppression of Irish agitation, Lalor's letters to the *Felon* were far more uncompromising than those he had written to the *Nation*, although they were based on the same legal premises. He called for the 'robber rule' of the 8,000 landlords to be broken, and his final article was a direct appeal for open armed rebellion. When the police raided the *Felon* offices, Lalor was away in Tipperary but he was eventually arrested near Nenagh and, after a short spell in prison there, transferred to Newgate Prison in Dublin. He was thus unable to take any part in the abortive 1848 rising at Ballingary, which led to the arrest and transportation of Smith O'Brien, Meagher, O'Donoghue and MacManus. John Martin and O'Doherty had already been transported, and Devin Reilly, another of Lalor's supporters, had fled to America. Lalor himself was not put on trial, but released from prison in November 1848 because of ill-health. Despite the transportation or exile of most of the leaders of Young Ireland, his desire for armed resistance was undiminished, and he wrote to Charles Gavan Duffy, whom he had met in person for the first time in Newgate Gaol, that the 'movement everywhere is running spontaneously into secret organisation, and I think *natural tendency* ought to be aided not interfered with'. He advocated a new journal as 'indispensable to any new movement', and urged Duffy to 'be at the head of it'. Duffy, who was still in prison, had discovered that Lalor's 'public letters were tame compared to his private exhortations and remonstrations', and declined his offer. Lalor therefore threw himself into the founding and administration of secret 'Felon Clubs', and began to plan a new journal of his own. This provoked the rivalry of Joseph Brennan, who, as editor of the *Irishman*, wanted no competing nationalist newspaper, and who began to oppose Lalor's influence in Dublin. Lalor failed to establish a paper, and Brennan seized the leadership of the Dublin Felon Club in the summer of 1849 while Lalor was away in the country.

But at last his wish for armed struggle was granted: a simultaneous uprising was planned for September 1849 in the counties of Cork, Limerick, Clare, Kilkenny, Tipperary, and Waterford, and Lalor was detailed to lead a raid on the barracks at Cashal. He spent a night lying out in preparation for the attack, but shortly after dawn concluded that his forces were inadequate, and he ordered them to disperse without firing a shot. In fact, he had 150 men at his disposal, enough to mount a credible action, and, besides, he had written only a year before that 'the first act of resistance is always, and must be ever, premature, imprudent, and dangerous'. Now he discovered the gap between war and warlike rhetoric, and his failure was made the more conspicuous by the courageous action of his rival Joseph Brennan, who led a vigorous if unsuccessful attack on the police station at Cappoquin. Lalor returned to Dublin, dispirited by the fiasco, and tried to revive his plans for a radical newspaper, but his always precarious health gave way for the last time, and he died after an attack of bronchitis on 27 December 1849.

IX

Lalor's legacy to Ireland was more symbolic than practical. He saw the big picture, but many of his details were vague and confusing. On one point, and it was the major point, he was right: he saw that the solution of the land question was of the greatest importance to Ireland and that any national movement which espoused that cause would be immeasurably strengthened. The combination of Parnellism with the Land League was to prove this correct. He also widened the nature of the debate on land tenure by examining the conditions under which the soil of Ireland had been apportioned, and the legal basis on which the landlords had exercised their rights.

But in many of his convictions and predictions he was simply wrong: he estimated that the retention of the corn crop would make the poorer Irish peasants economically viable, but this calculation, especially after the repeal of the Corn Laws, was extremely suspect; he said that Westminster would never curtail the rights of the landlords, but the numerous Land Acts in the second half of the nineteenth century, culminating in the massively interventionist Wyndham Act of 1903, proved this was incorrect; he thought the peasants were ready to rise in arms in 1848 and 1849, but they were not; he thought the Famine must result in the overthrow of the Ascendancy, but it did not; he thought that the small tenant-farmers must be protected or Ireland would be altogether destroyed, but in fact their disappearance in the Famine put the Irish economy on a sounder footing. Although Duffy had personal reasons for making Lalor appear more unworldly and impracticable than he was, there is more than a grain of truth in his portrait of him: 'His imagination was so vivid that his desires framed themselves like palpable images in his mind … He projected, as solitary thinkers are apt to do, in the unfenced fields of fancy, and his schemes seemed so logically exact and demonstrable that he could discern no difficulties which forbade their immediate execution. But when he tried to put them into action, they tripped over impediments of which he had taken no account.' Duffy in the Tenant Right League, Michael Davitt in the Land League, and William O'Brien in the United Irish League, took account of such impediments and they were to work out the details and organisation that Lalor had neglected. Although none of them were directly influenced by his ideas, his writing had prepared the ground for their work, for he had put the land question at the centre of the political agenda.

J.K.

JAMES FINTAN LALOR
Patriot & Political Essayist
(1807—1849)

JAMES FINTAN LALOR
Patriot & Political Essayist
(1807—1849)

BY

L. FOGARTY, B.A.

With a Preface by Arthur Griffith

DUBLIN

THE TALBOT PRESS LIMITED

89 TALBOT STREET

mar oilcuimne oeas-saeoil
oilis acá anois i ofiaiceas oé.

PRINTED 1918.
REPRINTED 1919

CONTENTS

PREFACE

The national demand for Repeal of the Union was degraded in the latter years of Conciliation Hall into a whine for " ameliorative measures" and the meaning of the noble term Moral Force distorted from passive resistance to despotism into passive obedience to tyranny. It is on his letters to the Confederate and Repeal Clubs, wherein under the name of " moral insurrection," he restored a true meaning to Moral Force, on his Letter to the Landlords of Ireland, and on his article on Tenant-Right and Land-lord-Law that Fintan Lalor's reputation as a thinker must rest.

After Davis, Mitchel, Duffy, and perhaps Father Kenyon, Lalor ranks as the most vigorous intellect of the Young Ireland movement; but he was rather in the movement than of the movement. The restoration of the soil to the peasantry was a greater ideal to him than the restoration of political liberty to the nation.

Repeal of the Union was to him sometimes a doubtful experiment, sometimes a question for the town populations—never a matter of concern to contrast with the settlement of the question of the ownership and possession of the soil. His indifference or opposition to Repeal did not spring from a desire for complete separation of the two countries. While he contemned Repeal and declared a dual monarchy impossible he favoured Federal Union. Ireland and England might bear the same relation to each other as " New York and Pennsylvania." But New York and Pennsylvania have a Washington above them.

Thus as a political thinker, Lalor failed: he knew little of history and less of political constitutions. As a writer he was often fallacious and sometimes contradictory, but the vigour of his style and the swing of his rhetoric concealed from many the occasional weakness of his argument. To an extreme shrewdness he sometimes united a childish simplicity as when he naively wrote that but for certain Young Irelanders who did not accept his views of the immediate policy " We could walk down the whole force

*of England in a month "—Ireland being then
divided, distracted, disarmed, and famished,
and England being then the strongest power in
the world.*

*His strength, his influence on his contem-
poraries, and his subsequent influence on Irish
movements came from his intense Agrarianism.
He flung the Agrarian question across the path
of the national movement and foretold ruin for
the latter if it did not link itself to the former.
Beside the Land question " Repeal dwarfed
down into a petty parish question" and deliverance from the bondage of landlordism was more
necessary than deliverance from the bondage of
foreign Government.   He believed the people
in 1848 would not fight for political liberty but
would fight for the land.   Events proved him
wrong—the nation was too weak and ill to fight
for anything, but he impressed Mitchel to a
degree with the belief that Agrarianism
could be used to promote the cause of political
liberty.   To Mitchel the question of the land
was a question to help Ireland to political
independence.   To Lalor the political independence was a question to help the peasantry to*

regain the soil. Both Mitchel and Lalor failed in 1848, but thereafter Nationalism and Agrarianism become closely identified and the Land League was the ultimate fruit of Lalor's creed and Mitchel's action.

The Land theory of Lalor resolves itself into the abolition of dual ownership and the creation of a peasant proprietary. His assertion that the ownership of the soil resides in the nation —a seemingly new and revolutionary doctrine in the Ireland of 1847—8—is a doctrine as old as the organised State. In Germany, Stein gave it practical effect in Lalor's boyhood when he converted the oppressed farmers of Prussia into owners of the soil. In his economic doctrine, Fintan Lalor nearly approached List, as when he argued that a prosperous and productive husbandry must be the groundwork of social economy and of a country; but he failed to apprehend, as List did, that Nationality was the highest value in economics, and that political liberty was the true security for social stability. The evil landlordism which Lalor regarded as worse than foreign Government was the child of foreign Government. The destruc-

tion of that foreign Government implied the end of its evil product. Lalor urged that the destruction of the evil would ensure the fall of English Government in Ireland. But even did it not do so, yet the greater end was secured —" the conquest" would have been repealed— the Irish people would have entered again into the possession of their soil.

Essentially, Lalor was a Land Reformer rather than a Nationalist. Had the Landowners of Ireland hearkened to him in 1847, they could have been to-day an accepted Irish aristocracy. They did not hearken, and forty years later his doctrine defeated them with ignominy. But though it liberated the Irish peasant from his serfdom on the soil it did not, as Lalor believed and declared it would, free the Irish nation. The key to that freedom lies in the doctrines of the man whom Lalor reverenced but whose vision was not his—Thomas Davis.

Ireland is the poorer because no collection has yet been made of the articles of Charles Gavan Duffy, John Mitchel and others in the " Nation " newspaper. Miss Fogarty has enriched Ireland by collecting the complete writ-

*ings of Fintan Lalor.   The article on the
"Rights of Labour," which is properly inserted
in the Appendices to this volume, and on the
strength of which attempts were made to show
that Lalor held Socialistic views was, however,
written by Thomas Devin Reilly.*

ARTHUR GRIFFITH.

March 21, 1918.

BIOGRAPHICAL INTRODUCTION.

The Seven Septs of Leix—The Lalor Family—The Tithe War and Patrick Lalor—Home Life and Schooldays of James Fintan Lalor—His Expedition to France—Character—Home surroundings—Relations with Mitchel—Events of 1848 and 1849—Influence on the Study of National Economy—Literary style—Peter Lalor, a Rebel Abroad—Effect of Lalor's Thought on Socialist Philosophers, on Davitt and the Land-Leaguers, Parnell, etc.—Modern Appreciations of Lalor—James Connolly's tribute.

When Oweny Mac Rory O'Moore, Chieftain of Leix, held his strongly fortified position in "the castled crag" of Dunamase, his name was one that struck terror into the heart of the invading Gall. Under his chieftainship the Seven Septs of Leix waged incessant warfare against the planter and settler, to whom their fertile acres seemed to constitute a standing invitation. Amongst these Septs were the forbears of the Lalor family, and of James Fintan Lalor, "the real Revolutionary of '48."

When Essex landed in Ireland, in the spring of 1599 with an army of 13,000 horse and 20,000 foot, he found O'Moore and his clans ready and eager for his coming. Of the famous Battle of the Pass of Plumes there are many documentary, and traditional accounts. There is no doubt, however that it was here Essex received the first of a series of " rude shocks " which made him abruptly abandon his brilliantly begun expedition to subdue the Munster Geraldines. Judging by his report written from Kilkenny immediately afterwards to Queen Elizabeth, and by the fact that he gave Leix a wide berth on his return march, two months later, it is clear that his forces suffered badly at the hands of the Seven Septs. To this day the borders of the road near Ballyroan—the scene of the conflict—are known as " Moinin na Fola."

The capture by O'Moore of " Black Thomas," 10th Earl of Ormond, and his subsequent release on handing over hostages to the value of £30,000, is an oft-told passage of Irish history. It may be remarked with regard to this incident, that the O'Lalours, with Keating, and the O'Kellies, were appointed to hold the hostages for their chief. It is recorded that after Owen's death the hostages (payment never having been made) were forced from them by the Lord Deputy, Mountjoy. At this time the O'Moores and the other Septs appear to have been at the zenith of their power. They repulsed the invader at every turn. The Deputy of the English crown had then to devise a new plan of conquest. The expedient was a simple one : the employment of starvation in lieu of military measures—a precedent acted upon in a later century with dire effect. The event known as " Mountjoy's harvest " is well described in the " Annals of the Four Masters." The Deputy marched with his forces into Leix, armed with spiked harrows, reaping hooks, and scythes. They cut down the green corn as it grew ; the portions of the crop that had matured they harvested and bore away. The fields, alien records say, were " well-manured and orderly fenced "

in spite of the long-continued strife. Mountjoy
revelling in the fiendish work, wrote to Carew saying:—
"I am busy at harvest, cutting down the honest
gentlemen's corn." In the wake of the "harvesters"
there remained a countryside ravaged and denuded
of the fruit of much labour, populated by starving
women and children.

Hard upon this incident followed the death of Owen
O'Moore from wounds received at the attack on
Ferney Abbey. Thereafter the lands of Leix fell for
the most part into the hands of settlers. But
even though the Septs were bereft of their haughty
and resourceful leader, they were not quelled. In
1607 (seven years after Owen's death) Mountjoy wrote
from Dublin to the English Privy Council to the
effect that the O'Moores and their fellow-rebels should
be banished into some remote parts of the other
provinces, being, "the notablest disturbers of the
peace of the kingdom, shooting at the recovery of their
lands taken from them for their rebellion and bestowed
upon the English."

Many deeds and documents were drawn up, many
meetings held, before finally the banishment of the
Septs was effected. With the O'Moores, the O'Lalour
clans were "transferred" into remote districts in
Kerry.

The agreement by which the Seven Septs were
transplanted was drawn up, and signed in the O'Lalour
townland—"Muileann O'Lalóur" now known as
"Lalor's Mills" in the parish of Maryborough. It
was drawn up by a certain Mr. Crosbie, a nominee
of Chichester—the then Lord Deputy; it included
numerous conditions, promises, and pledges, regarding
the remaining members of the transplanted septs, and

was formally signed and sealed by Crosbie. A MS. (extant in the Royal Irish Academy) from the pen of one of the banished O'Moores, tells how all these conditions were fulfilled. The survivors, relatives, and retainers of the septs, men, women, and children, were dispersed. For several days the officials of James I. were busily employed throughout Leix in " destroying the people remaining there, in seizing their cattle and all they possessed, while a savage order had been issued to hang any of them found in their ancient principality."

The members of the O'Lalour clans extirpated at this time numbered in all eighty-seven. Of these the chiefs were :—

> Hugh, and Domhnal Mac Seaghan O'Lalour.
> Donough and Hugh Mac Diarmuid O'Lalour.
> Domhnal Mac Theig O'Lalour.
> Donough Mac Domhnal O'Lalour.

Subsequently, when occasion offered, the men of Leix returned to their old territories : a hint of a rising was sufficient to rally them. After some time they gradually forced their way back to their home-country, and settled there.

Thus it was that Fintan Lalor's ancestors came to be in occupation of their holding at Tenakill (Tene-chell*) where in 1781 was born Patrick Lalor— destined to make the name famous for the first time in modern Irish history.

Like the men of his race who had with O'Moore risen eighteen times against the plantations, Patrick Lalor's was a mind restless in the presence of injustice.

---

* Formerly a castle and very extensive lands comprised the Tenechell townland.

A wrong no matter how long sanctioned by custom or tradition, was still a wrong calling to him, personally, for redress : insistent as any slogan peal it stirred the old blood in him. In 1831 he raised the flag and declared open the campaign against the Tithe system. Before it had well begun, a bribe was offered to Lalor —his strength recognised, the Tithe-collectors thought him worth " buying-off." But he refused. Thereupon the bailiff seized sheep on his farm to the value of the sum due to the local clergyman, a certain Mr. La Touche. The following day the owner recaptured his sheep by writ of replevin. After a few days an auction was called, but when the sheep were again driven from Tenakill they bore the word TITHE, in large pitch capitals on both sides. Branded thus, the sale of the sheep could not be effected in Mountrath, where they were put up for auction, and where the greatest excitement prevailed. On being transmitted to Smithfield Market the unlucky animals were taboo by the salesmen there—Patrick Lalor's salesmen having notified the others. Finally the sheep died from want and exposure on the road between Manchester and Leeds. So ended the first engagement in the anti-Tithe war—Lalor losing twenty-five of his sheep, and La Touche his tithes. It was a highly satisfactory result from Patrick Lalor's standpoint, as the whole countryside was thoroughly aroused, and the fight well begun. Once set on foot, the agitation continued until its culmination at Carrigshock—where " physical force " at length drew the attention of the English Parliament. The Tithe Commutation Act was passed in 1836, and the " mailed fist " of foreign rule pressed a little less heavily on the shoulders of the Irish peasant.

Patrick Lalor was returned as Member of Parliament for his native county at the famous election of 1832. He represented the popular interest as opposed to that of the landlord ascendancy. For many years he fought as one of O'Connell's " right-hand men " and was known in Conciliation Hall as " Honest Pat Lalor." But, like many another honest man, his " confidence in the Party " was ultimately shaken, and he retired into private life when he found that the Repeal movement was becoming less and less a great patriotic enterprise, and more a ladder to official distinction for a clique willing to compromise the nation's cause. Duffy's cryptic notes in the *Nation* on several Irish members holding seats in the House of Commons at the time of the General Election of 1847, include the following :—

" P. LALOR. An honest man. Retired in disgust." He had immense faith in the leadership of O'Connell. Many letters passed between them ; and the " Liberator," in one, expresses his sympathy with a father who had lost the support of his eldest son ! In fact, he refers to the " loss of " James Fintan in a tone that presumes the political, social, and eternal damnation of the youth.

When the Volunteers were revived by O'Connell in 1843, Patrick Lalor hastened to enrol himself, and like all the Irish Nationalists of that critical epoch, he anticipated, and held himself in readiness for, the *practical* fulfilment of many eloquent pledges. But the tide was not " taken at the flood " by the country's leader ; the opportunity passed and Ireland entered on the darkest years of her history. From this time may be dated Lalor's growing apathy towards Conciliation politics. It would seem that he was one of those to whom Fintan Lalor refers as to mistaking a certain "leaky collier smack" for a war-frigate, because "she hoisted gaudy colours, and her captain swore terribly." Moral force did not in fact claim very genuine admiration from Patrick Lalor—nor was the dividing line between his son's understanding of nationality, and his own, so rigidly marked. Going even farther, it may reasonably be urged that Young Ireland did not constitute a section, fundamentally distinct from the masses who followed the triumphant march of the Liberator during the previous decade. They understood, and were ready to give the one real proof of their loyalty to "that deathless thing"— Irish Nationality.

.   .   .   .   .   .

James Fintan, the eldest of Patrick Lalor's eleven sons, was born on 10th March, 1807. He was sent in 1825 to Carlow Lay College. Previously he had received some rudimentary instruction from private tutors. He showed a marked taste for classical reading, but won little prominence in the premium lists of the college. He seems to have turned away off the beaten track to examination fame, to foster the strong individuality that was to mark him as one in a thousand—nay one in a *generation* of progressive thought. To Plato and Diogenes, to Sallust, Cicero, or Juvenal he must have repeatedly turned. To English writers he had little recourse; Carlyle alone influenced him permanently. In late years Rousseau, Lamartine and contemporary writers in France claimed his attention. His most direct inspiration he owed to Wolfe Tone and Davis. " I have all my life suffered from a dearth of books," he once wrote; and it is clear from his work that except

these two great exponents of Irish nationality, no
previous writers moulded Lalor's thought on national
and economic questions.

Before leaving college he developed an aptitude for
the study of chemistry, and his father decided on
apprenticing him to Dr. Jacob, of Maryborough.
This plan had his mother's unqualified approval,
because it enabled her to enjoy frequent visits from
her favourite son. He took up his residence with Dr.
Jacob, and made it a custom to ride over to Tenakill
each Saturday, where he would remain till Monday
morning.

He was never idle. With hand or brain he worked
ceaselessly. When at Tenakill, he spent much of
his time in a low, attic-like chamber under the eaves
of the old house. Stuffed close with books and papers,
containing only a chair and desk, this study was something of a place of escape for Lalor from the household,
which, composed of so many small brothers and
sisters, was often disturbing. Here he was secure—
his mother solicitously shielding him from the annoy-
ance of interruption. His custom was to arise of a
morning at 3 a.m. and make his way to the river where
even in winter weather, he enjoyed a swim. Out
of his eleven brothers, Richard was his one chosen
comrade ; he, being the youngest, took no part in
Fintan's early life, and was excluded from the deeper
working of his brother's mind and imagination until
they were both adults. Thus even in boyhood, Fintan
Lalor was marked apart as one of the solitary ones of
earth—his thoughts exploring universes, his foot-
steps pacing the highways and byways of life, com-
panionless.

He ended his apprenticeship to Dr. Jacob very

precipitately, after having spent some eighteen months pursuing his chemical researches in Maryborough. He consulted no one as to ways and means, but embarked for France, where he knew he might at least count on experiencing " life." The horse kept for the purpose of the weekly visit to Tenakill, had to be sold to cover the initial expenses of the trip. It is needless to record Patrick Lalor's extreme displeasure at this step taken by his eldest son. It proved to be but one of many instances of Fintan's casting off the yoke of paternal authority.

His life abroad was a restless one. He was covetous of experience, action, adventure. The parts of France whose associations attracted him, he explored, quietly, with something of a devotee's ardour. Around the capital especially he found countless footprints which he followed with passionate interest, living the crowded days and months of 1789 over again. Though his tastes were not those of a *grand seigneur*, his travels cost a considerable sum, and but for frequent remittances from home, he might often have come to a stand-still. His mother, however, kept him supplied regularly—his father naturally refusing to encourage him morally or materially. No detailed information as to the friends he made—whether amongst " the wild Montagnards or respectable Lafayette-Lamartinists " is obtainable. We can not even assume that he met McDermott of *The Nation*, Leonard, or Daly, in Paris. All correspondence, diaries, and such-like documentary evidence met with the regrettable fate of all the effects of the felon, prior to the official call at his residence.

.   .   .   .   .   .

The famous election of 1832, in which the keenest

interest was taken throughout Leix and the bordering
counties, resulted in Patrick Lalor's return as member
for his county. The Lalor boys were all endowed
with wideawake minds, and the elder lads took an
active part in the campaign. Fintan wás then
twenty-five, and when this warfare of opinions opened,
was still abroad; towards its close he returned
to Tenakill. It is unlikely that his father's heading
the poll—"the people's man" in opposition to the
landlord interest—gave him any satisfaction whatever.
It was at this time his segregated life began, and his
philosophy assumed the definite outline future years
and occurrences were to strengthen and vivify.

Lalor has been represented as a "recluse, painfully
conscious of his physical defects"; as a miserable
being "cut off from social intercourse with all but his
next of kin." Such statements are exaggerated, and
give an entirely false notion of the real man. From
his birth he suffered from a disease of the spine which
impeded his growth; as his brothers were all well-built,
athletic, handsome, this contrast was all the more
painfully evident. In the latter part of his life he
suffered acutely from asthma; this complaint aggra-
vated by his imprisonment, was responsible for his
early death. To say that he was "cut off from his
fellows" is not at all a true assertion. Throughout
his native county he was immensely popular. Before
his work for the people began his father's fame had
been established as a staunch friend of justice and
fair play.

Years before he entered public life as leader-writer,
and joint editor of the *Irish Felon*, he had identified
himself with the Young Ireland workers. In the
outlying parishes and districts near his home he took

steps towards rallying and organising the young
men. A tiller of the soil, he was no stranger
amongst his peasant neighbours; on his advice,
backed by that of the *Nation* and the *United
Irishman*, they massed into clubs, and associations. For them, and with them, he worked;
their sufferings were his, and their wrongs
lashed his quick spirit to fury; for them he
defined in terms that could not be misunderstood, the
meaning of patriotism. To-day the sons of these
men will tell you how their fathers came together in
secret to learn the old faith from Lalor's lips. They
will show you where they buried their pikes, and
point out the thickets and " islands " in the bogs,
in which they lay concealed whilst red-coated hire-
lings tracked them. The tale of their outlaw lives,
of the barbarian tactics of their hunters whose orders
were " Let every man of the cursed papists swing ! "
is one that is only paralleled in the unwritten history
of the other provinces of Ireland. And as these men
of Leix pursue their story, the fact emerges that Fintan
Lalor was, in truth, the very reverse of what he is
often represented to have been—a monomaniac,
branded by nature and forced to live apart.

.   .   .   .   .   .

On returning from France, Lalor might well have
directed his efforts towards the founding of a school
of Political Economy for Small Nations. He might
have set about formulating theories of social equality
and propagated the doctrine of the fraternity of men.
But he did not ambition wide fame as a Revolutionary,
or world-reformer. So far, indeed, from raising his
voice to teach a continent just emerging from feudal
subjection, he turned his attention to the conditions

prevailing around him. He took up the work, that lay ready at his hand, and, individually faced the conflict of home problems—the evading of which had been the fashion with his class for centuries.

The system of Land Tenure then in vogue was part of the superimposed civilisation of the Gall, to which the Gael had never taken kindly. An alien version of civilisation, its whole code was inferior to the democratic, co-operative, spirit of the Clan System. Socially and economically, it meant progress in a backward direction. Lalor realised all this. He looked about and found his peasant neighbours chafing under this wilfully retrogressive influence : further, he saw that they had been brought to the lowest ebb of vitality by the poverty and humiliation it engendered. Then, he at once put his hand to the plough and began a work worthy of him—a man's work on behalf of his fellow-countrymen.

On January 11th he wrote his first letter to Gavan Duffy. He wrote with confidence and authority. The editor of the *Nation* circulated the letter amongst his colleagues, and requested Lalor to state his principles in the columns of the *Nation*. He admits being stimulated by " the startling programme " put forward by the unknown patriot ; but not yet sufficiently to abandon the rostrum, and come down to action. Had this letter been given immediate publicity ; had its note of warning been listened to by the Young Ireland leaders, it is not unlikely that much of the terrible and futile killing off of the people would have been averted.

During the ensuing months Lalor wrote constantly, vehemently, opening the eyes of many ; but stirring no section of the country into action. Most of his

letters were circulated among the Confederates, four,
only being published in the *Nation*. The spring and
summer months claimed a good deal of Lalor's time—
the work of his farm could not be thrown on younger
shoulders, nor could he, singly, take up the work of
the nation. The seasons of active business over, he
went, in September, to Tipperary for the purpose
of banding into a League the Tenants of that county.
He had communicated with Michael Doheny, and
assisted by him, convened a meeting at Holycross.
The call was answered, and a large crowd assembled.
Lalor, secretary to the meeting, read the resolutions
he had previously drawn up. Briefly, the objects
for which he desired to form this League of Tipperary
farmers, were : to assert the natural right of the
people to the land, the natural right of the occupying
tenants to a sufficient share of the crop they had
harvested, and to the seed that would ensure a sufficient crop for the following year. These objects
he set down clearly and logically in his resolutions.
He disliked eloquence, and relied on the naked weapons
of truth and justice, taking no pains either to explain
or persuade. To himself his plan of campaign, and
the theories on which it was based, were clear as
crystal ; to his hearers they sounded abstract—
scarcely intelligible. The impulse of the old school
(which dies with Parliamentarianism in Ireland)
towards flowery addresses, and speeches redundant
with strong and eloquent persuasion, was not a
mistaken one. A popular assembly, especially a rural
assembly, is almost always assailable by a wordy
fusilade. Condensed thought, born of quiet, calm,
solitary premeditation, leaves them cold.

Thus when Connor—" the Farmer's Friend "—

interrupted the meeting with a storm of eloquent abuse of everyone in general, but of Lalor in particular, his interruption was effective. His effort to defeat the real object of the gathering, and prevent the rallying of the Tipperary Tenants, was successful. He introduced a feeling of dissatisfaction with the resolutions, on the score of their vagueness and inadequacy. On a sand-grain of truth he erected an edifice. Why this uninvited speaker should have intruded to thwart the scheme of Lalor and Doheny, remains unexplained. It would be interesting to find if he actually undertook the journey from Dublin to Holycross out of pure " friendship " for the farmers.

This was Lalor's first and last effort to effect reform by what is termed " constitutional " means. Its failure does not seem to have daunted him, and it did not at all shake his faith in the people. Even a greater impediment than what Connor called " the dubious character of the resolutions " was the speaker's own personality. He had not the physique, the leader-like bearing, the glowing tongue, necessary to sway a popular gathering. And a fine sincerity, a singleness of purpose, a genuine impulse, did not help—nor do they usually help on such occasions. As Mitchel's letter to Smith O'Brien* explains, this Tipperary meeting was intended by Lalor to be the " thin edge of the wedge "—an initial step towards securing land-ownership for the people. He had also confided to Mitchel his intention of pursuing an active agitation on similar lines throughout the other southern counties.

The winter months of '47 passed, and of Fintan

* See Appendix 2 (c).

Lalor's public work at this time no record survives. It is possible that he lived quietly at Tenakill, and went occasionally with his brothers Thomas, Patrick, and Richard—who were members of the Confederation—to the neighbouring parishes to attempt something in the nature of organisation. But very little was actually done in these districts, until the following year. There was an appalling prevalence of physical debility and hopelessness, amongst the famine-weakened people : the demoralisation of the Poor Relief Measures had had dire effect. No one understood better than Lalor the awful condition of the peasantry ; no writer of the period felt it more personally, more acutely. The purest, and most highly gifted, people on the face of the earth held up as objects of public alms by those whose ingenuity and legislative foresight had brought about their destitution ! Infuriated, Lalor spoke out—spoke as one of them, not as one of " the selfish wrapped in their own padded safety " ; he could not restrain his impatience, or keep silent whilst they were misrepresented and apologised for. In the impassioned article with which he began his writing for the *Felon*, we learn something of what he endured personally, in the face of this widespread misery :—

> " From the robber rights and robber rule that have turned us into slaves and beggars in the land which God gave us for ours—Deliverance, oh Lord ! Deliverance or death—Deliverance, or this island a desert."

Until he joined Martin in continuing the publication of Mitchel's paper after the arrest of the latter in May, 1848, Lalor's name does not figure in the history of the period. Indeed it is difficult to credit him with silence and inactivity at this momentous time.

A traditional account has it that Fintan Lalor made a second journey to France, and was in Paris during the Revolution of February '48. Could this be definitely authenticated, it would explain both Lalor's lapse out of public life, and his failure to reply to Mitchel's letter of January 4th, 1848.* None of Lalor's letters from France during his first sojourn there have survived. He corresponded regularly with hism other, and with his favourite brother Richard but no communication from France *at any time* are available to verify verbal statements.

Discussions on the subject of Mitchel's debt to Lalor are futile. Every thinker and writer owes something to those who have thought and written before him. Mitchel is indebted to Lalor—if you will—just as Lalor is indebted to Caxton, the first English printer, or Caxton to the first Irish missionary in Northumberland, who taught the English the alphabet. Lalor inspired Mitchel, but he inspired equally all the Young Ireland intellectuals, and all subsequent Irish patriots, and all later writers on land questions. The two were men of genius. It is not possible to dig deeply enough, or widely enough, to find the first roots of genius, nor can its flame be followed to its ultimate reach into the Infinite. Mitchel and Lalor were men of creative mind; of ideas that germinate; of enthusiasm that enkindles. They had in common many characteristics; and on many points differed. They were, or could have been, completely complementary of each other. The one regret, the one disaster, the one germ of failure in

---

*See Appendix 1 (a).

them both, as in the movement for which they worked, sprang from the fact that they could not mingle forces in a common unity, for their common end. Neither had the facile quality which would enable him "to pull with" the other. Perhaps this argues a too strong sincerity in the one, a too strongly-felt individualism in the other—they could not, and did not work as colleagues. On all fundamental issues they agreed. Their appreciation each of the other's worth was genuine. No dispute, no positive disagreement took place between them; nothing kept them divided except the intangible, insuperable barrier nature had placed between their personalities.

Mitchel's letter to Lalor in January, '48,* and Lalor's words :—" John Mitchel, between whom and myself there was from the first an almost perfect agreement. May his fetters weigh light and his spirit live amongst us!" give a truer explanation of the attitudes of both than all the arguments and citations adduced by Duffy. If, indeed, Mitchel adopted Lalor's radical theory of land-ownership, he is to be admired; for only broad-minded men can be clearly convinced or completely converted. It lessens not at all the fame of men like John Mitchel and Parnell that they assimilated what was best and most serviceable of other men's ideas, and applied them to practical politics, rescuing them from sterility, using them as real and effective weapons.

This estranging element between the two great '48 men is explained away by a consideration of the defects in their respective characters. Lalor's fatal impatience—his dogmatic, exacting, and petulant impatience, must have made Mitchel treat him, on

*Appendix 1. See also Mitchel's letters to O'Brien (Appendix 2).

occasions, as a hot-headed schoolboy. Frank scorn
for men of less ability, courage, or enthusiasm, may
be admitted to have been Mitchel's one weakness.
The Até of the Greeks, which drew down vetoes of
doom from the gods, often possessed him, blinding his
fine reasoning faculties, making him the victim of his
own splendid passion. He never, in his published
writings, paid the slightest tribute to Lalor,
much as he respected him. Had he passed
away from the ranks of the active workers,
as Davis passed away, leaving a trailing glory
of memories behind, Mitchel's voice would have been
the loudest in eulogy. We are not surprised to find
him acknowledging his indebtedness to Davis, whom
he regarded as the real strength and inspiration of
the *Nation*. A recent writer* says :—" When we
think or speak of the Young Ireland movement our
thoughts go naturally and inevitably to those two,
Davis and Mitchel. The other men in the movement
are some of them brave figures, all of them honest,
but these two colossal figures overshadow them. And
in their personalities and their work they represent
exactly the two sides of the movement, Davis the
educational side and Mitchel the militant side."

Here is expressed precisely the greatness of Davis,
the strength of Mitchel. Lalor stands above the
reach of both, as he stands with them, making a triple
link of names to live on and redeem their age from
insignificance.

As patriot, and worker for the national cause, Fintan
Lalor is second only to Tone. He had not the poetic
sublimity of Davis ; but he had the grip of facts, the

* P. S. O'Hegarty in his Appreciation of John Mitchel.

stubborn will to get the better of difficulties, however small, sordid, tough. A tiller of the soil, he knew how to wrest from the heaviest clod its usefulness; he could meet the most uninspiring aspect of his enterprise with the same unflinching heart as the loftiest. He had not the soaring ambition that gave Mitchel his wings, but he had a far more practical head for affairs, for details, for organisation. Further, he had the preliminary advantage of being a democrat by birth, not by conviction. He knew his peasantry; he knew his "landed gentry" and although he may have overestimated the military prowess of the former, he never suffered from any illusions about the latter. When he first addressed the Landowners of Ireland, he wrote as one of the great body of the people, behind whom were ranged the strength of hand and soul, and of a single, common purpose. "You are far less important to the people, than the people are to you," he told them. In this instance his foresight amounted to prophecy. To Duffy it was folly to abandon "the thinking and educated classes and throw themselves (the Young Ireland leaders) on the support of the peasantry." To him "a commonwealth of sober-minded citizens" as distinct from a Republic of Marats and Robespierres like Mitchel and Lalor!—was the highest ideal of human government" and a "democracy of untutored peasants" the least desirable. Lalor had a first-knowledge of the peasantry: Duffy had not.

The history of Forty-eight is seldom told without a reference to "What might have been." Had the Confederation been formed three years earlier, had Davis lived, had the Dublin clubs effected Mitchel's rescue from Newgate, the Revolution might have been accomplished. The time invited. The hour seemed to have come—for all the other great European peoples it had come. " Old Earth was rocked by the storm-breath of democracy. That great Lazarus—the People had come forth from its tomb." Yet the revolutionary era passed leaving Ireland still an enslaved country, its territories occupied by aliens on a system more barbarous than that which existed in Prussia prior to 1811. Men like Lalor, Mitchel, Reilly, recognised the opportunity and were for immediate action. The other Confederates were, for the most part, men who deliberate, who venture slowly, who regard the moral responsibility of leadership as a thing to be feared—a thing almost beyond the capacity of ordinary humans. Mitchel believed in the will of the people—knowing that they awaited but the word. Writing to his kinsmen in Ulster, from a cell in Newgate, he said :—" I hear, just dying away, the measured tramp of ten thousand marching men—my gallant confederates, unarmed and silent, but with hearts like bended bow, waiting till the time comes. They have marched past my prison windows to let me know there are ten thousand fighting men in Dublin—' felons ' in heart and soul." Lalor too, believed in the people : he knew that their patriotism was an unconquerable strength. He knew that whatever else might fail their courage would not fail : that whoever was wrong, the instinct of the populace was not wrong. Long before the crisis, he wrote :—" The general population of this island are ready to find and furnish everything which can be demanded from the mass of a people—the numbers, physical strength, the animal daring, the health, hardihood, and endurance. No population on earth of equal power would furnish a more effective military conscription. We want only competent leaders—men of courage and capacity—men whom nature made and meant for leaders." Nature had not "made and meant for leaders" the Council as it then stood. The men who composed it were of all least likely to meet the crisis boldly. Not one of them had a practical policy; of all the Confederate leaders, thinkers, writers, Lalor *alone* had a practical, definite, formulated policy.

If the Insurrection failed as a practical issue, the "general population" did not cause its failure. In Cashel, Thurles, Wexford, Clonmel, beside Sliabh-na-mban, on the Quays of Waterford, forces actually rallied, imploring their leaders to give the word. In Dublin too, "the simple, faithful, common people" stood ready for the supreme test. Here it was on the night before Mitchel was hurriedly removed from Newgate, and shipped out of the country, that the rising had to be suppressed, almost by force. Of this incident Mr. Arthur Griffith remarks :—" There is no reason to doubt that an attempt to rescue Mitchel would have been a failure in its object. But there are occasions when it is wiser to attempt the impossible than to acquiesce."*

During the palpitating days of July and August, '48, Lalor was imprisoned, first in Nenagh gaol. afterwards in Newgate. Thus bound, gagged—forced to remain mute and inactive, at such a time, he suffered something beyond the measure of words. That his spirit survived unbroken is one of the best proofs of the man's heroic nature—the spirit that had prompted him to say :—" In cases like this the

---

* Preface to Doheny's "Felon's Track."

greatest crime that man can commit is the crime of failure." And the word " failure " must have reached him in a thousand rumours.

The long soul-searing months in prison left no mark on the man : his strength of purpose, his unwavering fidelity to, and firm belief in, the people's cause, survived. His health alone was permanently injured. He launched into a fresh journalistic enterprise ; and into what Gavan Duffy called " a new conspiracy." The newspaper project was carried out by Joseph Brennan, whose *Irishman* appeared early in '49. But Lalor's idea was to work out the plan conceived by the " Felons " while in Newgate, which was to be called the *Newgate Calendar**. It was to carry on consistently the policy of Mitchel's *United Irishman*, and of the *Felon*, and *Tribune*. It was also intended to propagate the most virile thought of the *Nation*, and Lalor sought to win over the Editor of that journal, for whom he had the very highest regard from first to last. Duffy seems to have given him but a lukewarm support : never a revolutionary at heart, he had by this time begun to set forth his brilliant Parliamentary policy from which, in later years, Parnell received an actuating impulse. The design of " a new conspiracy " he regarded as hopeless, and being hopeless, as *wicked*. Lalor did not think so.

He resided in Capel Street, Dublin. The personal influence he exerted at this time proved scarcely less powerful than that produced by his written words. A group of " good men and true " gathered around him, and to them he spoke revealing

*See Appendix 13.

an exceptional gift of easy, intelligible, en-
lightening discourse. Thus do the great men of
a generation fuse their souls into future generations
—leaving a definite stamp on the thought of succeeding years.

It was about this time John O'Leary and Thomas
Clarke Luby became intimate with Lalor. To them
he handed on the torch, thus linking the two great
national movements of the last century. They both
have left records of their supreme regard and reverence
for him, placing his name first on the scroll of the
immortal names of Forty-eight.

In September, 1849, the Conspiracy came to a
head. On the 16th of that month Lalor, with Brennan
Luby, Savage, and O'Leary, led a simultaneous rising
in the counties of Tipperary and Waterford. In the
neighbourhood of Cappoquin a considerable number
mustered. In the Tipperary districts the dearth of
resources and equipment forced Lalor and O'Leary
to abandon the attempt and disband their small
armies of insurgents. In Cappoquin, Brennan succeeded in an attack on the local stronghold of the R.I.C.
After this Brennan, who was blindly carrying out
Lalor's instructions, hesitated as to what his next
step should be. The delay meant disaster to the
hopes of his little following ; and in a short time they
were scattered, and Brennan was on his way to
America. Lalor and O'Leary returned to Dublin,
determining to give up the attempt *for the time*;
but "*the end was not yet.*" Lalor had an organised
scheme of action drawn up—a scientific, plan of
campaign. The other insurgent leaders acted on his
orders with implicit confidence. Order and organisation always appealed to him as the primary factors ;

unlike Mitchel he did not altogether see the necessity
for a fiery revolutionary impulse. In the previous
year Lalor wrote : " Oh, for one year of Davis now."
If he spoke out in the autumn of '49 he would have
said : " But for one hour of *Mitchel* now ! Lalor
could reason, plan, organise : Mitchel could goad
and infuriate popular feeling.

Although the Rising resulted in no victory, brought
the cause no nearer to success, yet to Lalor it meant
something gained. It gave him the opportunity he
desired to teach the country that the end of endeavour
had not been reached in Forty-eight : that to venture
nobly was better, almost, than to triumph. It was
his great opportunity for propagandist work. No
man could say that he did not prove his words, or
drive home the moral of his doctrine. By
this one move he checkmated the Fate that kept
him chained in Newgate whilst his comrades fought.
When, three months later, on 27th December, he died
from a more than usually severe attack of his old
bronchial malady, he had the satisfaction of knowing
that '49 had given the lie to the report of '48's failure,
as future generations should again give the lie to the
statement that Irish freedom had ceased to concern
Irishmen. On the occasion of his funeral (Sunday,
30th December) a procession four-deep, extending
the full length of O'Connell Street, accompanied his
remains to Glasnevin Cemetery.

Although it is not altogether true that " Lalor's
name and writings have been boycotted for more than
fifty years " ; it is true that they gained no recognition amongst Irishmen in Ireland. Until the late
D. J. O'Donoghue published in 1895 a small volume
of selections from Lalor's *Nation* and *Felon* letters,

no appreciable effort was made to renew their vogue, or revive their popularity in this country. Writers of distinction in America—Devoy, Boyle O'Reilly and Stephens, John Savage, Redpath, Ford, Carey, and in Scotland Murdock of Inverness, editor of *The Highlander*, gave ungrudging praise to the Irish economist. An English writer—P. H. Bagenal* claimed him as pioneer in the Land and Labour agitation, and the first of an incendiary band who united undeniable Irish talent with " the dangerous zeal of Paris communists ! "

Lalor's prose, from a merely academic point of view, has literary value. Its style alone should have won for it a place in the national literature, and given it a high status in the Universities of Ireland. It has much in common with the style of Carlyle ; it recalls Burke, Swift, Berkeley. The structure of sentence in Lalor is as nearly perfect as in many masters of the art of prose. Long explanatory sentences alternate with curt emotional ones : glowing, enkindling phrases give place to slow deliberate statements of facts, and logical self-evident deductions—all with a wonderful ease, a subtle grace and verve of movement. Sometimes engrossed so wholly with the *morale* of his work he emphasises, and repeats with a refrain effect. As Wagner, in certain lyrical moments, thunders aloud his theme with the full voice of his orchestra, so Lalor repeats his supreme subject with a clamorous insistence, employing all the hundred instruments of prose music. This is the witchery of art—the great soul-throb giving life, and strength, and power to the artist for all time.

. . . .

*See Appendix 9.

A Revolutionist in Russia may—for the moment—be honoured as a patriot in London, but certain it is that rebels in the English colonies are frequently singled out as recipients of royal favours : the careers of Lalor's colleague, Gavan Duffy, and of his brother, Peter, are instances of this. Fintan was bruised and tortured by the strong arm of English power in Ireland, because he dared to protest against its tyranny. Peter was twice offered a title by an English monarch, and given a statue to commemorate his fame as the Liberator of his fellow-colonists in Victoria, having first distinguished himself as insurgent-leader in the Ballarat gold fields. From digger to commandant of the insurrectionary forces ; from outlawed " rebel against Queen and country " to Parliamentary representative, and Speaker in the Legislative Assembly, his life was a singularly eventful one. He was more " conciliatory " in spirit than his brother, and far better versed in state-craft. The clue to his real character is given in the words of Raffaelo—an Italian who took part in, and wrote the history of, the Ballarat rising :—" Lalor, our leader, was an earnest, well-meaning, no-two-ways, non-John Bullised, Irishman." It is also worth recording that on the two occasions when Queen Victoria offered him a knighthood, he respectfully declined its acceptance.

No monument stands to the memory of Fintan Lalor, in any town or village of his native county. One has been raised to the memory of a Viscount de Vesci, whose national " work " chiefly consisted in drawing an immense income from the land appropriated by his ancestors in Leix : it confronts the stranger on his approaching Abbeyleix from the railway station.

It is not, however, in dead stone and marble that the memory of Ireland's patriots live.

. . . . . .

Lalor was the first Irishman who wrote on the subject of political economy from a national standpoint. Since, many European economists have so treated the science—notably Karl Marx and Friedrich List. From Lalor originated the theory that land belongs of right to the people who till it ; and that private property in land is an evil custon justified neither by time nor usage. The *fact* is old as truth itself—yet the Irish thinker was the first to put it down in black and white. He stated it plainly, leaving to later writers its re-statement, development, and elaboration.

Standish O'Grady says, of this aspect of Lalor's work, " James Fintan Lalor was the first who preached that the nations own the land, a doctrine of which Europe will hear much in the coming century, for whether it be true or false, the world must assuredly face it as the old wayfarer had to face the Sphinx." To estimate Lalor's value—to give him a place merely as a " political-economist," as some writers have endeavoured to do, is to make a false start. For " political economist " the title " social-economist " or national-economist " must be substituted. He would himself eschew all commerce with *politics*. Nationality, he worked for : political enterprise he despised. In Ireland it is not uncommon to find the two ideas opposed—a nationalist being everything a politician is not. " Political rights," wrote Lalor, " are but paper and parchment. It is the social constitution that determines the condition and character of a people—that makes and moulds the life of man."

His work in the field of national economics he subordinates to his larger enterprise—the independence of the nation. He states this with clearness ; the agrarian movement has value for him chiefly as a means to the nobler end. By concentrating on the point of Tenant Right, he was forging a weapon, with which the fight for Independence should be carried to a successful issue.*

John O'Leary, in a short memoir of Lalor, pays a just, if brief, tribute to his ability as a clear thinker and writer. But he inaccurately particularises Lalor into a school of " Politico-economists " : in truth he bulks too large, and towers too high to be *placed* in any arbitrary manner. A similar fallacy entered into the controversy begun in the Lalor Centenary number of the *Irish Nation*. Whether Lalor was primarily *Nationalist, Economist,* or *Socialist* was variously urged. Each writer wished to give him a distinct " label," and say the final word.

Before coming to the consideration of the modern exponents of Lalor's economic teaching—Davitt and the Land Leaguers—we encounter a name of considerable importance : that of Henry George.

A San Francisco printer, Henry George is best known as the author of " Progress and Poverty." Within eighteen years of its first appearance 4,000,000 copies of this book were sold, and it was translated into many European languages. Henry George advocated collectivism in the true sense, and gave more than a hint to the modern promoters of organised Guildism. He

---

*See concluding paragraphs of Letter to the Irish Confederate and Repeal Clubs.

attacked the system of private property in land, setting forth its destructive and far-reaching effects with clearness and vigour. For this he deserves recognition, and may be said to have inaugurated a movement which is the strongest force in English and continental politics to-day. But to accord him the additional merit of originality is not justifiable. The new doctrine of which George was said to be the prophet, was the old faith of an Irish felon.

The biographer of Henry George describes a picturesque ride through a forest during which the journalist received a flash of inspiration. " He saw in a moment," the story runs, " that speculation makes artificially scarce land, on which, and from which all men, barbarous or civilised, farmers, timber-cutters, miners, or dwellers and workers in towns and cities must live—thus compelling labour and capital to pay, not the comparatively low price for its use but an extremely high artificial price." All this the philosopher learnt as his morning ride led him through the vast, beautiful, but to humanity *en masse*, useless, tracts of prairie and wood. It is easy to argue that inspiration gives birth to the wisdom of the poet : it is far less credible that economic truths spring from a like source.

Henry George began life as a printer on the staff of the *Alta*, a Californian journal. Later he took up reporting, and soon attained to a place on the *Irish World*, then under the editorship of John Boyle O'Reilly. Though the author of " Progress and Poverty " is above the accusation of mere plagiarism from the pages of Fintan Lalor, he never *admitted* having adopted what John O'Leary terms " Lalor's peculiar views on the land question." He may have set up the type to print some letter from the *Nation* or *Felon* ; or he may have read, and forgotten having read, one of the many American republications of them. A germ, at least of the Irish patriot's philosophy had invaded his subconscious mind prior to the appearance of his book in 1879 ; and when he published, two years later, his pamphlet on the Irish Land Question, he proves his thorough acceptance of Lalor's views. It is also evident that Michael Davitt, who alludes frequently to " my friend Henry George," gave the brilliant American a schooling in Irish national economy. In 1878 Davitt was pursuing an active campaign in America. Fintan Lalor contributed his texts ; and the realities of peasant oppression, personally experienced, lent vigour and fire to his words. The *Flag of Ireland* and the *Irishman* circulated them throughout every part of the States.

The democratic mind of Henry George was soil receptive for the fall of the seed the Land Leaguers scattered. He understood the universal nature of the problem underlying that of landlord tyranny in Ireland. Like Lalor, he grasps its world-wide significance, and regards landlordism as the worst kind of capitalism. " Mankind will yet be masters of the earth," wrote the Irishman in '48. " The right of the people to make the laws, this produced the first great modern earthquake whose latent shocks even now are heaving the heart of the world. The right of the people to own the land—this will produce the next. Train your hands and your sons' hands, gentlemen of the earth, for you, and they, will yet have to use them." This principle was expounded by the American, and

given a wide currency in many European languages.*

Had the two writers belonged to the same country
and written contemporaneously, they might often
have stood on the same platform. They agreed on
many fundamental questions, but Lalor would reject
many of the theories advanced by George. There
in no denying Lalor's strong attitude on the land
question ; and as a social democrat he stands firm.
But it is not unlikely that he would be one of those
who uphold that "Rebellion against society and
advocacy of humanity run counter."

The surest sign that a man thinks the opinions of
another sound, is his adoption of them in so whole-
hearted a manner as to repeat them on many occasions
in his own words. If years elapse before a lesson
impresses itself forcibly enough to be re-expressed and
thundered over continents, its inherent truth is all the
better proven, its universal application all the more
firmly established. It was not until after his release
from Dartmoor in December, 1877, that Michael Davitt
began to make practical use of the dogma expounded
by Lalor in '48. Previously, in the years 1835 and 1836,
Sharman Crawford had brought forward Bills in the
British House of Commons which aimed at the better-
ment of the conditions of the Ulster tenantry. Both
Bills were dropped. A decade later he established a
Tenant Right Association in his native county of
Down. Thus Sharman Crawford may be said to have
antedated Lalor by drawing attention to the slavish

* "Private property in land blocks the way of advancing civilisation" ("Progress and Poverty," Bk. VI. et passim). For com-
parisons between the writings of Henry George and Fintan Lalor,
see Appendix 5.

conditions under which the tenants held their lands
Yet a wide gulf separates the petty policy of Crawford,
from the broad principles Lalor set down. In the
first place, Sharman-Crawford was merely concerned
with the tenants of Ulster, whose conditions and
tenures were not at all those of the other Irish provinces. Secondly: the logical end of Crawford's
highest aim would mean a system of partnership
between landlord and tenant. Thirdly: he argued
from the assumption that the Garrison, or landlord,
class held the land by a right other than " the robber's
right." Fourthly: he appealed to the British Legis-
lature.

Isaac Butt, *not* Davitt, continued the work of the
founder of Ulster Tenant right. Like him he held
firmly to " constitutional " weapons, and lived to
prove their worthlessness. Butt called his policy
that of " the Three F's." When Davitt began the
Land War proper, this policy, like that of Duffy's
Tenant League of North and South, were ruthlessly
brushed aside. They failed, as half-measures in
Ireland always fail. Fintan Lalor's principles
triumphed. Precisely on the lines he laid down, the
Land War was carried on by Davitt. " A new force
was to be created which was to be actively renewed
more on the lines of Fintan Lalor's principles than on
those of Duffy. . . It was to be a joint evolution
of Fenianism and Home Rule," thus wrote Davitt
on the launching of " The New Departure," as his
Land League movement was first termed. Again he
writes :—" What was wanted was to link the land or
social question to that of Home Rule, by making the
ownership of the soil the basis of the fight for self-
government. Tactically it would mean an attack

upon the weakest point in the English hold on Ireland in the form of a national crusade against landlordism, while such a movement would possess the additional advantage of being calculated to win a maximum of auxiliary help from those whom the system had driven out of the country." If for " self-government " we substitute " independence," and for " auxiliary help " " reliance on ourselves alone," we lay bare the self-same idea expressed by Lalor in his second letter to the *Felon*. Davitt pursued his campaign with signal success. He won the strenuous and unwavering support of the country. He lent a high personal courage, a vehement zeal, a dauntless devotion to his cause. Up to the anti-climax of the Kilmainham Treaty every prospect indicated a sweeping and decisive victory for the people.

Parnell inclined, from the outset, to agreement with Lalor and Davitt on the land question. Working along different lines, he purposed to win to the same goal. Parnell " the embodied conviction " of Ireland's nationhood—the sole unbribed survivor of years of English political life—regarded the question of land reform as subsidiary to that of Home Rule. To him it was not a vital national problem of real and pressing urgency ; he interpreted it as something like a bone of contention between two classes. Later, indeed, he acknowledged with Davitt that it signified a great deal more. But the " divine discontent "—with which Lalor was familiar in his day—the stuff out of which the red-hot steel of revolution is forged, was unknown to the great Separatist statesman : Lalor only would strip and " bid Ireland strip " on this issue.

Thus was the Land War waged : thus, all but triumphantly won. The " land for the people "

D

gained, a reign of agricultural prosperity began. The genius of Lalor had proved the lightning flash through the clouds. But this prosperity re-acted strangely on the spirit of the country : an aftermath—the last Lalor would have forecasted, followed. That which Padraig Pearse described as " the one sickening chapter in a story which has everywhere else some exultation of pride," was opened.

It is hard to excuse or explain away " the failure of the last generation," the apathy of a people who, having secured their immediate mercenary ends loosened their grasp on all else. Was it indeed the age-old episode—the mess of pottage accepted, the golden heritage bartered ?

The name of Fintan Lalor was never spoken : Mitchel's, Tone's, and Davitt's became as half-forgotten myths. Nationality appeared a lifeless thing, of no account or value. What '48 recognised as a lever to move towards Independence, 1903 conceived as the Be-all and End-all of hope. Parnell's contemptuous statement that " Land-ownership and loyalty are generally inseparable with a peasantry no way prone in any country to care or sacrifice much for the principle of patriotism " took on the appearance of a mere truth, rather than a diplomatic dictum uttered in the presence of enemies. Later, Canon Sheehan pronounced even sterner judgment :—" It will be found that the more comprehensive idea of Irish nationhood has always been cherished by the dwellers in the towns and cities of Ireland. To them Ireland has been a whole, a homogeneous entity to be welded more and more until it took on the consistency of a nation. The people of flocks and herds can only conceive of patriotism as it affects the land."

But the nemesis that pursues English misrule in Ireland followed. The spiritlessness of the country proved a superficial phase. It passed with the inevitable motion that belongs to things in a natural sequence. The modern renascence of national vitality, the renewal of self-reliance and racial pride, reached the heart of the people ; and the old gods to which Sinn Fein won them back, found them ready for homage and sacrifice.

Fintan Lalor knew his fellow-countrymen better than the later thinkers ; *his* judgment of them was grounded on a faith and sympathy which passing phases could not deceive. " A secure and independent agricultural peasantry is the only base on which a people ever rises or can be raised, or on which a nation can safely rest." Thus he wrote in 1847, and to-day the proof of his wisdom is before us.

Not for fame nor personal prestige, but for his country's honour, Fintan Lalor wrote, and laboured, and spent his meagre hoard of health. Though it has often been half said, half acknowledged, it is undeniably clear to us, who are the heirs of his ideals and achievements, that he was the dominant mind inspiring his age. Of that tragically eventful period he alone took a high aim and a firm stand.

James Connolly, one of the noblest martyrs for the creed of Irish Nationality, and gallant fighter for Labour's emancipation, wrote of James Fintan Lalor :—

" He died as he had lived, a revolutionist and a rebel against all forms of politic and social injustice. . . . . In his writings, as we study them to-day, we find principles of action and of society which

have within them, not only the best plan of
campaign for a country seeking its freedom through
insurrection against a dominant nation, but also the
seeds of the more perfect social peace of the future."

L. FOGARTY.

James Fintan Lalor

TO CHARLES GAVAN DUFFY,.

EDITOR OF THE " NATION."

TINAKILL, ABBEYLEIX,
January 11th, 1847.

I am one of those who never joined the Repeal
Association or the Repeal Movement—one of Mr.
O'Connell's " creeping, crawling, cowardly creatures "
—though I was a Repealer in private feeling at one
time, for I hardly know that I can say I am one now,
having almost taken a hatred and disgust to this my
own country and countrymen. I did not join the
agitation, because I saw—not from reflection, but
from natural instinct, the same instinct that makes
one shrink from eating carrion—that the leaders and
their measures, means, and proceedings, were intrinsi-
cally and essentially vile and base ; and such as never
either could or ought to succeed. Before I embarked
in the boat I looked at the crew and the commander ;
the same boat which you and others mistook in '43
for a war-frigate, because she hoisted gaudy colours,
and that her captain swore terribly ; I knew her at
once for a leaky collier-smack, with a craven crew to
man her and a sworn dastard and forsworn traitor
at the helm—a fact which you and Young Ireland
would seem never to have discovered until he ordered
the boat to be stranded, and yourselves set ashore.

I would fain become one of the " National " party,
if they could consent to act along with me and I

1

with them.　But I confess I have my many doubts—
I have had them all along ; and they have been terribly strengthened by the two last numbers of the
Nation—I mean those of December 26 and January
2 ; the last (January 9) I have not yet seen.　It is
not figure, but fact, that reading those two numbers
made me ill.　I have long been intending to write to
you to resolve those doubts, and have only been
prevented by sickness.　I must now defer doing so
for some little time longer, and my reason for writing
the present hurried note is this : It has just occurred
to me that at the meeting on Wednesday, an Association may possibly be formed on such a basis, and
resolutions or pledges adopted of such a character,
as would exclude and excommunicate me and many
beside.

These resolutions or pledges may relate either—
1st to the end ; 2nd to the means.　Now remark—
1st, as to the end :—Should the end be defined strictly,
in terms or effect, to be Repeal, simple Repeal, and
nothing but or besides Repeal, I would thereby
be excluded.　For, in the first place, I will never
contribute one shilling, or give my name, heart, or
hand, for such an object as the simple Repeal by the
British Parliament of the Act of Union.　I shall state
my reasons hereafter, not having time now.　Don't
define the object, nor give it such a name as would
define it.　Call it by some general name—independence
if you will—and secondly, I will never act with, nor
aid any organisation limiting itself strictly to the
sole object of dissolving the present connection with
Britain and rigidly excluding every other.　I will
not be fettered and handcuffed.　A mightier question
is in the land—one beside which Repeal dwarfs down

into a petty parish question; one on which Ireland may not alone try her own right, but try the right of the world; on which she would be, not merely an asserter of old principles often asserted, and better asserted before her, an humble and feeble imitator and follower of other countries—but an original inventor, propounder, and propagandist, in the van of the earth, and heading the nations; on which her success or her failure alike would never be forgotten by man, but would make her, for ever, the lodestar of history; on which Ulster would be not " on her flank," but at her side, and on which, better and best of all, she need not plead in humble petitions her beggarly wrongs and how beggarly she bore them, nor plead any right save the right of her might.

And if the magnitude and magnificence of that other question be not apparent and recognised—any more than the fact that on its settlement now depends the existence of an old and not utterly worthless people—it is partly, indeed, because the mass of mankind see all such questions, at first, through a diminishing glass, and every question is little until some one man makes it great; but partly also, because the agitation of the Repeal question has been made to act as a proscription of every other. Repeal may perish with all who support it sooner than I will consent to be fettered on this question, or to connect myself with any organised body that would ban or merge in favour of Repeal or any other measure, that greatest of all our rights on this side of heaven— God's grant to Adam and his poor children for ever, when He sent them from Eden in His wrath and bid them go work for their bread. Why should I name it?

National independence, then, in what form of words you please ; but denounce nothing—proscribe nothing—surrender nothing, more especially of your own freedom of action. Leave yourselves free individually and collectively.

2nd. As to the means :—If any resolution or pledge be adopted to seek legislative independence by moral force and legal proceedings alone, with a denunciation or renunciation of all or any other means or proceedings, you may have millions of better and stronger men than I to join you ; but you won't have me. Such pledge, I am convinced, is not necessary to legalise any association. To illegalise there must, I conceive, be positive evidence of act or intention—deeds done or words spoken. Omitting to do anything can surely form no foundation for a legal charge. What ! Is silence a proof of criminal intention ? I speak, of course, in ignorance, being no lawyer, thank God. But whether I be correct or not, I never will subscribe or assent to any such pledge or resolution, as regards the use of none but legal means—any means and all means might be made illegal by Act of Parliament ; and such pledge, therefore, is passive obedience. As to the pledge of abstaining from the use of any but moral force, I am quite willing to take such pledge if, and provided, the English Government agree to take it also ; but, " if not, not." Let England pledge not to argue the question by the prison, the convict-ship or the halter, and I will readily pledge not to argue it in any form of physical logic. But dogs tied and stones loose is no bargain. Let the stones be given up ; or unmuzzle the wolf-dog. There is one at this moment in every cabin throughout the land, nearly fit already to be untied—and he will be savager by-and-by. For Repeal, indeed he will never bite, but only bay ; but there is *another* matter to settle between us and England. There has already, I think, been too much giving in on this question of means and force. Merely to save or assert the abstract right for the use of other nations or other times won't do for me. We must save it for our own use, and assert it too, if need be, and occasion offer. You will receive, and, I hope read this on to-morrow morning before the Committee meet. My petition to you is that you will use your influence to prevent any of these resolutions from being adopted, which would cut me off from co-operating with the new Association, should one be founded. Don't mention my name. It is one not worth half a farthing ; but such as it is I don't wish to give it to the Seceders until I have some better guarantee than I possess as yet that their new organisation will be anything better, stronger, or nobler than a decently conducted Conciliation Hall, free from its open and brazen profession of meaness, falsehood, cowardice and corruption, but essentially just as feeble, inefficient, and ridiculous.

Is there any apology needed for addressing you in this manner ? I don't know. Perhaps I have no right ; though I have been a seceder since I ceased to be a child. I owe to you some gratitude. *You have given me a country*. Before your time I was an alien and an exile, though living in my own land. I hope you won't make me one again.

This letter has been hastily written ; and I have not acquired the faculty of expressing what I wish with clearness or facility. Still I hope you will understand, or at least that you will not misunderstand me. The *Nation* of last Saturday might possibly give me information which would render my writing plainly unnecessary; but I don't receive it until Wednesday, being in partnership with another person.—I remain, your obedient servant,

JAMES F. LALOR.

To Charles Gavan Duffy.

A NEW NATION.

Proposal for an Agricultural Association between the Landowners and Occupiers.

To the Landowners of Ireland.

TINAKILL, ABBEYLEIX,
April 19.

I address you, my lords and gentlemen, from a great distance—the distance that separates you from the people—for I am one of the people. This is a disadvantage of some account, and might be discouraging at a season more settled. But I know that in periods of peril, when distress and disaster are present, and danger and dread are in the future, men are allowed to assume rights which must lie in abeyance during ordinary times This is my reason and right in addressing you—that I am excited and authorised by the feelings and emergencies of the occasion. This is my claim to a hearing. Not that I ask it in my own cause or in that of the class I belong to ; not that I urge it for sake of the masses of men who are unable to ask it for themselves ; but that I claim a hearing and crave to be heard on your own behalf—on behalf of your own interest, and honour, and existence, as owners of that soil on which thousands now are famishing to death for want of food.

My general object in addressing you is that of calling public notice, if I can, to the full extent of the effects which I think must inevitably follow fast on present events, if the course of those events be not checked or changed. All the facts I possess I have considered and

7

counted in one view together, in their connexion and consequence, and inferred the result. This is a task which few others, I fear, have undertaken, nor is it any matter of surprise. Within sight and sound of this dismal calamity, amid the actual horrors of every passing hour, it is scarcely possible to look far into the future, or take thought and care for remote results. In the presence of famine men are blind to its effects. It is doing its work in the dark, and no watch is set or warning raised. From every house and every voice throughout this land there is but one cry now— the cry for food. Food for to-day and for to-morrow —for this year and the next. But not all the clamour and outcry that has been raised throughout Ireland during the last few months has added a single pound to the supply of food either for this year or the next. What men were unable to do, they set about doing ; what they were able to do, they left and are leaving undone. For something else is wanting, and requires to be provided, besides food for to-day or to-morrow— else a revolution is at hand. A revolution of the worst type and character—not such as when a nation breaks up under armed violence, to re-unite and rise on structure as strong as before ; but such as when it falls in pieces, rotting to a final and fætid ruin.

Beside the general object mentioned, I have a particular and more definite purpose, which will develop itself as I proceed. It would be useless to state it formally before it can be fully understood. Though I write more especially for you, my lords and gentlemen, landowners of Ireland, yet I write also for the public ; and shall address myself to either, as occasion may seem to demand.

The failure of the potato, and consequent famine,

is one of those events which come now and then to
do the work of ages in a day, and change the very
nature of an entire nation at once. It has even
already produced a deeper social disorganisation than
did the French revolution—greater waste of life—
wider loss of property—more than the horrors, with
none of the hopes. For its direction still seems
dragging downwards, while her revolution took France
to the sun—gave her wealth, and victory, and renown
—a free people and a firm peasantry, lords of their
own land. It has unsettled society to the foundation ;
deranged every interest, every class, every household.
Every man's place and relation is altered ; labour has
left its track, and life lost its form. One entire class,
the most numerous and important in Ireland, has
already begun to give way ; and is about being dis-
placed. The tenant-farmer of ten acres or under is
being converted into an " independent labourer."
But it is accomplishing something more than mere
social derangement, or a dislocation of classes. It
has come as if commissioned to produce, at length
and not too soon, a dissolution of that state and order
of existence in which we have heretofore been living.
The constitution of society that has prevailed in this
island can no longer maintain itself, or be maintained.
It has been tried for generations ; it has now, at least,
been fully and finally tested ; and the test has proved
fatal. It was ever unsound and infirm ; and is now
breaking to pieces under the first severe experiment,
an experiment which that of any other country would
have easily withstood. Nor heaven nor human
nature will suffer it to be re-established or continue.
If the earth, indeed, with all things therein was made
wholly for the few and none of it for the many, then

it may continue ; if they be bound to submit in patience to perish of famine and famine-fever, then it may continue. But if all have a right to live, and to live in their own land among their own people ; if they have a right to live in freedom and comfort on their own labour ; if the humblest among them has a right to a full, secure and honest subsistence, not the knavish and beggarly subsistence of the poor-house, then that constitution cannot and it shall not be re-established again. When society fails to perform its duty and fulfil its office of providing for its people ; it must take another and more effective form, or it must cease to exist. When its members begin to die out under destitution—when they begin to perish in thousands under famine and the effects of famine—when they begin to desert and fly from the land in hundreds of thousands under the force and fear of deadly famine—then it is time to see it is God's will that society should stand dissolved, and assume another shape and action ; and he works his will by human hands and natural agencies. This case has arisen even now in Ireland, and the effect has already followed in part. Society stands dissolved. In effect, as well as of right, it stands dissolved, and another requires to be constituted. To the past we can never return, even if we would. The potato was our sole and only capital, to live and work on, to make much or little of ; and on it the entire social economy of this country was founded, formed and supported. That system and state of things can never again be resumed or restored ; not even should the potato return. A new adjustment is now to be formed, is to form and develop itself ; a new social order to be arranged ; a new people to be organised. Or otherwise that people itself is about to become extinct. Either of these is inevitable ; and either is desirable. In condition and character and conduct, a stain to earth, a scandal among the nations, a shame to nature, a grievance to Heaven, this people has been for ages past—a dark spot in the path of the sun. Nature and Heaven can bear it no longer. To any one who either looks to an immediate directing Providence, or trusts to a settled course of natural causes, it is clear that this island is about to take existence under a new tenure ; or else that Nature has issued her decree—often issued heretofore against nations and races, and ever for the same crime—that one other imbecile and cowardly people shall cease to exist, and no longer cumber the earth.

The power of framing a new order of arrangement is in your hands, my lords and gentlemen, if you choose to exercise it. The work of reconstruction belongs of right to you, if you have the wisdom and the will to do it. It is in emergencies and occasions like the present, rather than in ordinary and settled times, that a national aristocracy is required ; and if they be not worthy of such occasions, they are worthless altogether. It is a time like this that tries and tests the worth of a class, as it tests the worth of individual men. Not to time should the task be committed, nor to chance ; not to the government of England, which is incompetent to the case ; not to the parliament of England where you are made a mark for pelting at ; nor to the desperate remedies of men whom you have, yourselves, made desperate. Ireland demands from you now something more than her present dole of daily food—a mode and system of procuring full food for herself. She looks to you for this—that she be

not condemned to live as a beggar on public alms,
nor as a pauper on public works and poorhouse rations ;
but aided and enabled to find or form a mode of making
her own bread in all future time by free, unforced,
and honest labour.   She has lost her means of living ;
she requires some other, more sufficient and secure
than those she has lost.   Her demand, in full and fine,
is for what is of more effective worth and weight than
all the political constitutions that were ever fashioned ;
for what senates or sovereigns cannot make or unmake,
but men must make for themselves—her demand is
for a new SOCIAL CONSTITUTION under which to
live.   This is the task you are called on to undertake—
the work you are wanted to do, or forfeit your footing
in this island of ours—a work to which political constitution is little in comparison and light in importance.   Political rights are but paper and parchment.
It is the social constitution that determines the condition and character of a people, that makes and
moulds the life of man.

We are now living in the midst of a social anarchy,
in which no man knows with certainty what he is,
or what he can call his own.   Never was government
or guidance more necessary to a people ; but government or guidance there is none, for the one great
purpose needed.   An extreme and extraordinary case
has arisen—one that seldom arises in modern times—
and not to be treated by any ordinary law.   A new
structure of society has to be created ; and the
country has a right to require of you to counsel, and
conduct, and lead her ; because you own her soil ;
because your own worth and value are in question—
your own interest and position involved and committed ; because the work cannot so speedily and safely

be done without your aid ; because in some respects
and in some degree you are considered chargeable
with the calamitous crisis that has occurred ; because
your rights of ownership are thought by numbers to
be the main or only obstacle to the creation at once
of a sound system of social prosperity and happiness,
which would be formed by the natural energies and
social instincts of mankind, if those energies were left
free to act, and not fettered or interfered with by
your claims of dominion ; and finally because you
ought of right to be where you have never chosen to
be—at the head of this people. And at their head
or at their side you must now stand, or your aid will
not be taken. On other terms it will not now be
accepted ; and the work will be done by other hands
than yours. You are far less important to the people
than the people are to you. You cannot stand or act
alone, but they can. In the case that has arisen
the main power is in their hands, the little in yours.
Your power of position has departed. You cannot
reform and re-organise a whole people without their
consent and co-operation. You cannot act against
them—you cannot act without them. They can do
what is wanted of themselves and without your
assistance. They have the will and may learn the
way. A dissolution of the social system has taken
place. The failure of the potato was the *immediate
exciting* cause. Into the *predisposing* causes it is
needless for the present to enquire. There was no
outrise or revolt against it. It was not broken up by
violence. It was borne for ages in beggarly patience,
until it perished by the visitation of God in the order
of nature. A clear original right returns and reverts
to the people—the right of establishing, and entering

into a new social arrangement. The right is in them because the power is in them. The right lodges where the power lodges. It is not a case to which governments or parliaments are competent. The sole office and duty of government under the circumstances is that of supporting the destitute, and maintaining public order during the period of transition, and rê-organisation. Should it attempt doing more than this, it will be assuming a power which it does not possess, and cannot even make an effort to exercise without committing injustice, doing injury, and suffering defeat. With the great body and mass of the people, in their original character and capacity, resides of necessity the power, in its full plenitude, of framing or falling into a new form of organisation— a new mode of living and labour. Your aid, my lords and gentlemen, is most desirable, if accorded on terms, and in a mode which would be thought likely to contribute to general benefit and happiness. On other terms or for other objects—with a view to your own personal interests alone, and on terms to assert and secure your own position at any cost to the country and community—if offered on such views and terms, your service and aid will not be accepted ; and the present condition of anarchy will be protracted by strife and struggle, terminating possibly in violent convulsion, from which you, at least, would come out the losers, whoever might be the winners. To ensure against such a contingency it is necessary that you should now combine and co-operate with that people from whom, for long ages, you have stood apart, aliens and enemies to them as they to you. They count more in millions than you count in thousands. If you desire that they and you should now join

hands to carry the boat over the rapids, it must be on
terms which they will accept ; on terms of advantage
to them as well as to you—and the first condition and
very basis of a union must be the distinct acknowledg-
ment and assertion, in its widest extent, in its fullest
force, power, and plenitude, of the principle of ALLE-
GIANCE TO COUNTRY. On any other basis no
federation can form or be formed to take effect or be
of force in Ireland now. To save mistake I ought
to mention, and mark what it is I do not mean, as well
as what my meaning is. I do not mean that you
should declare for Repeal. I scarcely know that
I can call myself a Repealer, further than this—
that I would not say aye to the question if it were
put to me to decide. The results of Repeal would
depend on the means and men by whom it should have
been accomplished. It might give to Ireland all that
Ireland wants, and withering in want of—equal liberty,
and equal laws, science and art, manufacture and trade,
respect and renown ; wealth to the merchant, security
and comfort to the cottage ; its pride of power and
place to the castle, fame and fortune to genius and
talent, all of that which ennobles and endears to man
the land he lives in—this it might do. It might
subject us to an odious and ignoble tyranny. I am
far from wishing you to take any course that would
pledge you to Repeal, or to any other political
measure. I do not write with a view to Repeal, or
any other political object whatever. My meaning is
far more general, and states itself in more general
terms. Nothing is requisite or required that would
commit you in particulars, to any political party,
cause, or course of conduct.

But a full act and avowal of attachment and

allegiance to this island, in priority and preference to any and every other country—this is required, and will be strictly required; not in mere idle form of protest and profession, but in full efficient proof and practice. That Ireland is your own mother-country —and her people your people—that her interest and honour, her gain and her glory, are counted as your own—that her rights and liberties you still defend as part of your inheritance—that in peace you will lead her progress, and carry her banner in battle—that your labour shall be in her service, and your lives laid down at her need—that henceforth you will be not a foreign garrison but a national guard; this you must declare and adopt, as the principle of your proceeding, and the spirit of your action, and the rule of your order; for these are the duties of nobility Adopt this principle, and you are armed; on it is your safety and your strength; the future is fettered at your feet, and your name and race shall flourish and not fail. Ireland is yours for ages, yet on the condition that you will be Irishmen, in name, in faith, in fact. Refuse it, and you commit yourselves, in the position of paupers, to the mercy of English ministers and English members; you throw your very existence on English support, which England soon may find too costly to afford; you lie at the feet of events, you lie in the way of a people, and the movement of events and the march of a people shall be over you. Allegiance to this fair island; it is your title of tenure to the lands you hold, and in right of it you hold them. If you deny and disown it you assert another title, and must determine to hold your inheritance by force, at your own will and to our injury, in despite and defiance of us and ours for ever.

This would be a bootless and feeble insult, and dangerous withal ; for your title is worth little indeed under the law you would appeal to : that while from Ireland you take rank and revenue, blood and birth and name—everything that makes home, and binds to country—you yet look not to her, but to another land, for home and country ; that you desert and disown, if not hate her old native people ; that in England are your hearts and hopes, and that all your household gods are English. This crime is charged to you : unjustly charged I trust it is—for a worse crime, and more infamous than disloyalty or treason to kings or crowns is disloyalty or treason to country. It is a crime not made by lawyers, but made by God ; a crime against nature itself—against all its laws, affections, interests, and instincts. Yet the charge is not made against you without colour of truth and show of reason. On every question that arises, in every contest and collision, whether of honour or interest, you take side and cause with England. All blame for this does not rest on you ; but some of it does. Much and most of it rests on a class of men whose claim to attention, however strong, I must defer to a future letter. All such ground of charge must be removed and renounced. For ever, henceforth, the owners of our soil must be Irish. To all who own land or living in Ireland, Ireland henceforth must be the Queen-island. She holds in her hands the hostages for their fealty, and will not longer put up with TREASON. On no other common ground or general principle can a federation take place between the nobles of the land and the nation at large, than that of common faith and fealty to this their common country.

The formation of the Irish Party was hailed at the time by many as one step of a movement in the direction of Ireland. It may perhaps, indicate a change of ideas, ·if not of feelings. You have probably begun to find out that if your feelings are English, yet your fortunes are Irish ; that Ireland's peril is perilous to yourselves ; that in renouncing your country and adopting another, you renounce and revolt from the laws of nature ; and that nature herself is strong enough to punish the treason. You have, moreover, got some slight cause to doubt whether England esteems your attachment as of any value, your interest as of much importance, or your very existence as worth the expense and peril of supporting. But we recognise nothing Irish in this party except its name ; nothing that can entitle it to command or call round it the hearts or hopes of this people ; or raise it to any higher position than that of a mere club and a petty club, formed by a class for the single object of saving its own little interests from injury, at any cost to the country. Whether for its professed or its private objects, shelter as an Irish party or as a landowners' club, it is equally and utterly inefficient, and can do nothing for the salvation of the country or for yours. It excludes the people. It embraces no great public principles, passions, purpose, or policy. It bears no banner, and shows no motto. It rallies no support, and inspires no confidence ; proposes nothing, and promises nothing. To resist the minister, should his measures of relief or improvement be deemed injurious to the landowners—this appears the sole object of the Irish Party. But your claims as landowners are no longer maintainable or defensible on their own merits and means. To maintain, you must connect them with those of your country. A union between parties of the same class— a union of landowners with each other is adequate to no purpose now. The union required is a union between all classes of whom the people is composed. You are powerless without a people beside or behind you. You must call the commons into your council; and make their private interests and public objects—nay even perhaps their public passions—a part of your policy. The Irish Party must expand and enlarge into the Irish people ; or another, and more effective Association be framed.

To organise a new mode and condition of labour— a new industrial system ; to frame and fix a new order of society ; in a word, to give to Ireland a new social constitution under which the natural capacity of this country would be put into effective action ; the re-sources of its land, labour, and capital developed and made available ; its slumbering and decaying ener-gies of mind and muscle excited, directed, and em-ployed ; and the condition and character of its people reconstructed, improved, and elevated ; this I have already stated is the general object which now calls for the united action of the landowners and people of Ireland in association assembled. The energies of nature and action of time, working together in their wonted course and current, will indeed, in long or short be adequate, without aid or effort of ours, to form a new and effective settlement of society ; but the fabric thus formed will be raised out of the relics, and rest on the ruins of the present existing people in all classes. For their own safety and preservation it is necessary that all those classes should now combine to take the direction of that revolution which will otherwise effect itself, and which indeed is in actual process of being effected without their consent, control, or guidance. That position has become too perilous to maintain. Your path of safety, as well as of honour, is now the public highway. No bye-way of your own will carry you through the perils that beset, and the greater perils that are before you. There are many and important questions at issue between you and the landholders, between you and the labourers, between you and the people, between you and other classes of the people, between those classes among themselves. No government, no legislation, no general statutes, no special statutes, no power on earth but the parties concerned, no mode on earth, save that of voluntary agreement, can settle those questions. Why should we not meet and settle them amicably ? Leave them not to be settled by time, or to be settled by strength.

What to create a complete and efficient industrial economy ; to form and give force to a new state and mode of existence ; to organise and animate, and put into healthy vigorous action that complex living machine, a social system ; to frame and adjust the fabric of society in its mightiest proportions and minutest parts with all its vast and various interests, arrangements, orders and conditions, independent, yet involved, conflicting, yet co-operating—what to do all this ? A work impossible to man ; and which, in extent, or detail, he never yet undertook or attempted to perform. A work of which the theory and principles are beyond his knowledge or discovery, and the practical execution beyond his utmost power. Nature has reserved it to herself, to effect by a process of her own, for which no artificial process was or can be substituted with success. A work we cannot do, God's hand alone, not man's, can do it. True—and neither can you form in all its parts the smallest plant that grows. But sow the seed and the plant forms. The powers of vitality but require to be set in movement, and the contrivances of nature left free to act. Even so it is in the case we consider. That work may be done, and *you* must do it or others will; and you must do it at once for it cannot be waited for. Nor is it, when examined, an undertaking that need dazzle or daunt by its magnitude or multiplicity, the meanest mind of all amongst us. It includes no such complication of difficult questions as it may seem to ; and the only question actually involved is one easy of settlement, when put into comparison with its apparent mass. Its theory contains itself in a single principle ; its practical solution is comprised and completed in a single operation. Lay but the foundation and the work is done. Lay the foundation ; nature effects the rest ; society forms and fits itself, even as the plant grows when the seed is sown. Lay deep and strong the only foundation that is firm under the foot of a nation— a secure and independent agricultural peasantry. A secure and independent agricultural peasantry is the only base on which a people ever rises, or ever can be raised ; or on which a nation can safely rest.

A productive and prosperous husbandry is the sole groundwork of a solid social economy. On it and out of it springs the mechanic, and artisan, and trading dealer ; fed and fostered by it these swell into the manufacturer and merchant, who multiply into merchants and manufacturers ; sustained by it still, these enlarge, and gather, and solidify into

companies, corporations, classes—into great manufacturing and mercantile systems and interests, which
often, like unnatural children, disown and desert
the mother that bore and the nurse that fed them ;
without it there is neither manufacture or trade—
nor means to make them, for it is agriculture alone
that furnishes those means. Food is our first want—
to procure it our first work. The agricultural class,
therefore, must precede and provide for every other.
It is first in order of nature, necessity, and time. It
is an abundant agriculture alone that creates and
sustains manufactures, and arts, and traffic. It is
an increasing agriculture alone that extends them.
For it is the surplus of food it accumulates, after
providing ordinary subsistence, that forms new wants
and demands, and the modes and means to meet and
satisfy them. Such is the actual process ; a process
that never yet was reversed, or carried out in any
other course or order ; so it was at first, and so will it
be for ever—in every time, in every clime, in every
country. Adopt this process ; create what has never
yet existed in Ireland an active and affluent husbandry,
a secure and independent agricultural peasantry, able
to accumulate as well as to produce—do this, and you
raise a thriving and happy community, a solid social
economy, a prosperous people, an effective nation.
Create the husbandman, and you create the mechanic,
the artisan, the manufacturer, the merchant. Thus
you will work on the ordinance of God, in the order
and with the powers of nature. All the natural motives
and means with which man is endowed will come then
to your relief and assistance, and do the rest. Any
further interference with the course and process of
natural laws would be useless and mischievous.

Neither monarchs nor mobs ever yet were able to manage or modify that natural process with success ; or ever attempted to enforce interference without doing grievous injury and gross injustice. The abortive and mischievous legislation of both old and recent times affords lessons enough of this, if we choose to learn them.

There seems to be a vague impression on a large portion of the public mind of this country that national attention and exertion, as well as individual effort, should be directed into a course the reverse in its steps and stages of that natural order which I have pointed out. We are in the habit of hearing it asserted that a large development of manufacturing industry is what Ireland needs, and that to establish it should be her chief objects. It is even assumed, not unfrequently, that a manufacturing system must precede, and is the only mode of promoting, the improvement and prosperity of agriculture itself. This is an error I could wish to see abandoned. It distracts effort and attention from the point on which both ought to be directed, and on which they could act with effect. I am prepared to prove—what, indeed, any man may prove to himself—that neither by the private enterprise of individuals or companies, neither by the force of national feeling anyhow exerted, neither by public association or public action of any kind or extent nor by government aid, if such aid could be expected— neither by these or any other means and appliances can a manufacturing system be established in Ireland, nor so much as a factory built on firm ground, until the support of a numerous and efficient agricultural yeomanry be first secured. Good friends, you that are recommending us to encourage native manu-

facture and to form manufacturing associations;
tradesmen and townsfolk of Ireland will you cease to
follow a phantom, and give hand and help to create
such a yeomanry ?

My general object, the formation of a new social
economy thus resolves itself into the formation of a
a new agricultural system. The principles on which
that new system is to be founded must either be
settled by agreement between the landowners and
the people, or they must be settled by a struggle.
What I think those principles ought to be, if they be
made articles of agreement, as well as the practical
mode of arriving at and arranging such agreement,
I shall take another opportunity of stating.

You, however, my lords and gentlemen, it would
appear from your present proceedings, have already
settled among yourselves the entire future economy
of your country—determined the fortunes and fate
of this entire island—disposed of the existence of this
little people of eight millions. The small landholdings are to be " consolidated " into large farms, the
small landholders " converted " into " independent
labourers "; those labourers are, of course, to be
paupers—those paupers to be supported by a poor
law—that poor law is to be in your hands to manage
and administer. Thus is to be got rid of the surplus
of population beyond what the landowners require.
Meantime, by forcible ejectments, forced surrender,
and forced emigration, you are effecting the process
of " conversion " a little too rapidly, perhaps for
steady and safe working.

And so, it seems, you have doomed a people to
extinction and decreed to abolish Ireland ? The
undertaking is a large one. Are you sure your

strength will not be tested ? The settlement you have made requires nothing to give it efficacy, except the assent or acquiescence of eight millions of people. Will they assent or acquiesce ? Will Ireland, at last, perish like a lamb and let her blood sink in the ground, or will she turn as turns the baited lion ? For my own part I can pronounce no opinion ; and for you, my lords and gentlemen, if you have any doubts on the question, I think it would be wisdom to pause in your present course of proceeding until steps can be taken and measures adopted for effecting an accommodation and arrangement between you and the present occupiers of the soil, on terms that would preserve the rights and promote the interests of each party. If you persevere in enforcing a clearance of your lands you will force men to weigh your existence, as landowners, against the existence of the Irish people. The result of the struggle which that question might produce ought, at best, to be a matter of doubt in your minds ; even though you should be aided, as you doubtless would be, by the unanimous and cordial support of the people of England, whose respect and esteem for you are so well known and so loudly attested.

I have the honour to remain, my lords and gentlemen, your humble and obedient servant,

JAMES F. LALOR.

TENANTS' RIGHT AND LANDLORD LAW.

" I may be told that this famine is a visitation of Divine Providence, but I do not admit that. I fear there is blasphemy in charging on the Almighty the result of our own doings. . . . . . God's famine is known by the general scarcity of food of which it is the consequence. There is no general scarcity, there has been no general scarcity in Ireland, either during the present or the past year, except in one solitary species of vegetable. The soil had produced its usual tribute for the support of those by whom it was cultivated. . . . The vice inherent in our system of social and political economy is so settled that it eludes enquiry. You cannot trace it to the source. The poor man on whom the coroner holds an inquest has been murdered, but no one killed him. Who did it? No one did it. Yet it was done."

I have just now seen in the *Nation* of last Saturday, May 1, the foregoing extract from the lecture of Dr. Hughes on the " Condition of Ireland."*

Doctor Hughes does not seem sufficiently to understand how the failure of a single root can have produced a famine. " The vice of our political and social economy is one that eludes inquiry." But is it indeed so obscure? Has it then been able to conceal or disguise itself? It must be dragged out. In self-defence the question is now forced on us, whether there be any particular class or institution specially chargeable? It is a question easily answered. Into the more remote causes of the famine it is now needless to enquire, but it is easily traced back to its immediate origin. The facts are few, and are soon told and speedily understood, when the conditions of the country it had to act on have first been stated. I state them from recollection; I have no returns

---

* For context, see Appendix 4.

at hand to refer to, but I shall be found generally correct.

There are in Ireland, or were last year, 231,000 agricultural families, comprising 319,000 adult male labourers, depending altogether on wages for subsistence. If I commit any mistake, it is that of overstating the number of such families. There was not constant employment to be found for those 319,000 men, and the rate of wages was very low. The labourer, partially employed and poorly paid, was unable, on the mere hire of his hands, to feed himself and those who looked to him for food. He borrowed for six months (May 1 to Nov. 1st) from some neighbouring farmer the use of a quarter of an acre of land. He paid for this six months' use the sum of £2 12s. 6d. The farmer, however, manured the land ; he manured it by paring off with the plough a thin layer of surface, which the labourer left to dry, made up into heaps, and burned into ashes, which he spread over the ground. On the land so manured—for in no other mode was it ever manured—he planted potatoes, and was so able to live ; and he did live on, from year to year, from youth to grey hair, from father to son, in penury and patience. Whether the penury made the patience, or the patience made the penury, I stay not to enquire. Certain it is that they commonly go together. The details I am giving are sufficiently well known here, but I write for England. Such as I state him is, or was, the Irish labourer, that " independent labourer," whose free and happy condition is now offered and recommended so strongly to the small landholder, as preferable to his own. Last year this man did as usual. He planted his potatoes ; but when he came to dig them out there were none

to be digged. Two hundred and thirty thousand
families began to die of hunger ; and famine ran wild
into fever.

The cultivated soil of Ireland is distributed, or was
last year, into about 880,000 landholdings, each occupied by a family. Of this number of landholders,
510,000 were in occupation, each of farms varying in
size from one acre to ten, and none of them exceeding
that extent. This class of men differed little in the
appearance, but very much in the reality of circumstance and condition, from the class of men labourers.
Their circumstances varied with the size of the holding ;
but the lowest family among them stood far above
the labourer. Their means of subsistence were somewhat greater, their securities for subsistence were far
greater. They did not, as the labourers did, commonly starve or suffer hunger through the summer
months—the *famine months* as we call them in this
country. Those of them who held farms of from five
to ten acres of holding enjoyed some little share of
the comfort of life, which the careless and mirthful
temperament of Ireland heightened into happiness.
The men dressed well on Sunday, and the women
gaily, at least in all parts of the country with which
I am acquainted. The smallest landholders of this
class were labourers also—labourers with allotments—
labourers with assurance against positive starvation.
Each man had at least a foothold of existence. Each
man had potato-ground at least ; at a high rent,
indeed, but not so high as the one-acre rent. Still,
however, the lowest grade of these men were miserable
enough ; but not so utterly so as the mere labourer.
Their country had hope for them too, while she had
none for the labourer. To avoid if I can, confusion

or complication of statement, I put out of view for
the present the holdings of size beyond ten acres each,
amounting in number to about 370,000. But
such as I state it was the condition, so far as affects
the small occupiers I speak of, in which the famine
found Ireland.

Two circumstances of this man's situation, and those
not unimportant, remain yet however to be stated,
in account for the past, and in calculation for the
future. One of them is, that he held his land by no
other assurance, legal or moral, than his landlord's
pecuniary personal interest in retaining him as a tenant. He had commonly no lease of his holding, or,
if he had it was rendered null in effect by numberless
circumstances which I cannot stop to state. The
feelings that exist in England between landlord and
tenant, coming down from old times, and handed
on as an heirloom from generation to generation—
the feeling of family pride, the feeling of family
attachment, the habit of the house, the fashion of the
land, the custom of the country, all those things that
stand for laws, and are stronger than laws—are here
unknown ; as, indeed, they are beginning to decay
and die out in England. But the working farmer
of Ireland who held his own plough, and acted as his
own labourer, was able to pay a higher rent for his
land than the farmer of any other class ; and hence
alone he continued to hold it. This was his title of
tenure—his only title ; his security against the grazier
and against the extensive tillage farmer ; his sole
security for leave to live.

Such is the first circumstance requiring note. The
second is this :—The occupier I speak of, if his holding
was very small, put the entire of it in tillage ; if large

F

he put a portion in pasture. In either case his tillage ground was appropriated to two crops—a potato crop and a grain crop. He sowed grain for his landlord, he planted potatoes for himself. The corn paid the rent, the potato fed the tenant. When the holding was small, the grain crop was insufficient, alone to balance rent; a portion of potatoes made up the deficiency by feeding a hog. When the holding was larger, the grain crop was often more than sufficient, with the help of a hog, to clear rent and tithe rent, and county rate and poor rate. In such cases the cultivator had a small overplus, which he could actually dispose of as he liked, and he commonly laid it out in the purchase of mere luxuries, such as shoes, wearing apparel, and other articles of convenience. So stood the landholders of ten acres or under.

Last year this man did according to custom. He planted potatoes for his own support, he sowed corn for his landlord's rent. The potato perished; the landlord took the crop. The tenant-cultivator paid his rents—was forced to pay them—sold his grain crop to pay them, and had to pray to man as well as to God for his daily bread. I state general facts; I stop not to count scattered and petty exceptions. Who is it says the landlords got no rent last year? Bernal Osborne says so—and adds that the conduct of the Irish farmers in withholding their rents was most disagreeable and discreditable, and disgraceful. One hundred voices and pens have said and repeated it. The landlords are in parliament and in the " Compositor's room " ; the tenant-cultivators are not. The lion is no painter. It may be so that in districts of Tipperary the tenants, or many of them, kept their corn for food—thus paying themselves for their labour, capital, and seed, and saving their own lives—instead of paying the land rent. It may be said that in those districts the full rents were not paid ; it may be said that in Galway, Mayo, Cork, and elsewhere they *could not* be paid. The oat crop failed partially, as the potato failed wholly ; and when these were the crops in the ground the landowner, of course, in many cases lost a portion of his rent, as the tenant-cultivator lost his entire provision of food. But these exceptions are inefficient against the facts I state. I say and assert that the landowners took entire possession of last year's harvest—of the whole effective sum and substance of that harvest. The food for this year's subsistence, the seed for next year's crop—the landlord took it all. He stood to his right, and got his rent—and hunger was in five hundred thousand houses, pinching dearth in all, deadly famine in many. Famine, more or less was in five hundred thousand families ; famine, with all its diseases and decay ; famine, with all its fears and horrors ; famine, with all its dreadful pains, and more dreadful debility. All pined and wasted, sickened and drooped ; numbers died—the strong man, the fair maiden, the little infant—the landlord got his rent.

Relief committees were formed and public works set on foot. The landowners grew bustling, if not busy, in the work of demanding relief and dispensing it. To the local relief funds very many of them, indeed, contributed nothing ; but there were others who contributed even so large a sum as 000.000$\frac{1}{4}$ per cent. on their annual income, and were most properly appreciated and praised as beneficent individuals, while several gave a percentage of double or thrice

that amount—and Ireland rang with applause. They
demanded the Labour Rates Act ; called for works
which would increase the productive power of the
soil ; and grew clamorous in the expression of pity
for their suffering countrymen, whom they charged
government with delivering up to famine by adopting
an erroneous and insufficient system of relief.   Finally
under the flag of their country, they met in the
Rotunda, and formed an Irish party for the professed
object of establishing and supporting an Irish policy
for Irish purposes ; that is to say, for the purpose
of taking care that the pecuniary interests of the
landowners of Ireland should suffer no detriment,
more especially by any extension of poor law relief.
Such is the history of the present famine.   Does it
furnish or suggest an answer to the concluding query
of Dr. Hughes ?

But another famine is in preparation, and will
surely come, no matter for fallacious statements of
an increased breadth of tillage.

The lord of the soil had got his rent, and become a
public and professed patriot.   The cultivator of the
soil had lost his provision of food, and gone out on the
public roads, for public wages.   The preparations for
tillage were, of course neglected.   The tenant had
neither seed nor subsistence ; or, if he had any small
provision of either, he was soon deprived of it by the
relief system.   Whatever seed he might have saved
from the landlord ; whatever little means he possessed for making manure ; whatever small capital
was in his hands to work on with, were taken from
him by relief committees and relieving officers.   The
law was laid down, and acted on very generally, that
no man should obtain either gratuitous relief or

public employment until he should first be completely pauperised. If he had seed corn, he should consume it, if he had a cow he should sell it—and not a few of them said, as they are still saying, " if he had land he should give it up " ; otherwise he could have no title to relief. This was to say, they chose rather to maintain wholly for ever after the first few months, than to maintain partially for those few months ; rather to give permanent support than temporary aid ; rather to create a pauper than to assist a struggling worker. This was to declare in favour of pauperism, and to vote for another famine. I am putting no blame on the parties to this proceeding. The reasons for it were plausible in appearance. I am merely stating a fact, and charging nothing more than mistake. " We must guard against the evils," said the official authorities " of indiscriminate relief, and avoid the risk of pauperising the feelings of the peasantry, encouraging the spirit of dependence, and training them to the trade of beggars." To me it seems it would have been safer to incur the risk of pauperising *their feelings* than the certainty of pauperising *their means* ; and better even to take away *the will* to be independent than to take away *the power*. " When there are such numbers utterly destitute," said the relief committee, " why should we give a man relief who has a barrel of oats in his possession ? It would be wasting silver and cheating *the poor*." What was it to them that the barrel of oats, if kept for seed, would have produced 12 barrels at harvest ?—a return of 1,200 per cent., on the cost of feeding the man while consuming his poor little provision of corn seed.

The tenant was left without seed or substance. The

effect is, that the smaller class of holdings remain
uncropped and untilled, and in many cases abandoned. This class of holdings constituted a large
portion of the tillage lands of Ireland. The largest
class of farms are exclusively under grass. The
proportion of pasture diminishes as the farm grows
smaller. The smallest class of holdings are exclusively in tillage ; and these are not in the usual course
of preparation for being cropped, but will, to all
appearance of evidence remain waste this year. The
season is passing. The potato will not be planted
to any efficient extent. No adequate substitute has
been adopted or found—no adequate additional
quantity of corn crop, or of any crop has been sowed,
or is in course of sowing. A famine for next year is
all but secured. Numbers of the small occupiers
have surrendered their holdings. The landlords are
assisting the natural operation of the famine instead
of arresting it—putting the tenant out of his foothold
of land instead of aiding him to retain and cultivate
it. In every district the tenantry are being evicted
in hundreds by legal process, by compelled surrenders,
by forced sales for trifling sums—the price being very
frequently paid by a receipt for fictitious or forgotten
arrears. These men are being converted into " independent labourers " ; and the number already evicted
will form a very considerable addition to a class too
numerous even now for the demands or resources of
the country—too many to be absorbed—too many to
be supported. Another famine comes next year—a
a famine of undiminished powers of destruction to
act on diminished powers of resource and resistance—
a famine of equal origin to act on weakened conditions. Additional numbers of the small occupiers are

thrown out of occupation of land—the entire body
I am speaking of are thrown out. It will not stop
short of that, or stop even there. Who can limit
such an operation to ten-acre holdings, or limit it
at all ? They lose this land ; they acquire, in lieu of
it, that valuable species of Irish property, " independent labour." Stop one moment to look at the
fact. Five hundred thousand families added to the
two hundred and thirty thousand who form the
present mass of labour—six hundred and seventy
thousand adult males converted into " independent
labourers "—six hundred and seventy thousand hands
added to those three hundred and nineteen thousand
already so successfully engaged in independent labour.
But surely I overstate. No one will believe this can
happen until it has actually happened. No one
believes in the future—no one sees to-morrow as he
sees to-day. I may not be correct to the very last
figure, but I am effectively correct. But is it I that
say this result will come—is it I alone ? Every
speaker in Parliament whose words carry weight
forestates this result, defends, justifies, urges it ; and
not a voice rises to protest against the principle, the
feasibility, the consequences. It is the policy and
purpose of every act that is passing through the legis-
lature. " Whereas it is desirable that the conversion
of the inferior classes of Irish landholders into independent labourers shall take effect as speedily and
safely as possible, and without serious damage or
danger to the English interest or the English garrison
in Ireland." I read this as the preamble of every Irish
act of the session. It is assumed and set down that
such conversion is to take place—not partially neither,
but universally. No authority assumes, no argument

asserts, that the small occupiers are *too many*, and
ought to be reduced. The assertion is that the small
occupier is a man who ought not to be existing. He
ought to be, and is henceforth, an independent labourer.
No cause, moreover, is operating against one of the
class that is not operating against all.

But the confiscation will not be limited to ten-acre
holdings. There are causes in operation which will
render it impossible for tillage land to pay as high a
rent as land under grass. Many causes—some
natural, others artificial—render it impossible to
produce corn in this country at as low a cost, quality
for quality, as it can be produced in most others.
Our corn will soon be undersold in the market by a
superior article—a result rendered surer and speedier
by the present increased demand for foreign corn.
Shortly too, the house-feeding of cattle can no longer
be carried on. Even if the repeal of the corn duty
should realise the utmost expectations of its advocates, and if there should be, consequently, a propor-
tionate increase in the demand for beef, mutton,
butter, and wool, yet the tillage land of Ireland
turned into grass land, will be fully adequate to
supply the increased demand. House-feeding will
be unable to compete against grass-feeding, or to pay
for itself. Together with corn, therefore, the root
crops will no longer be raised ; a regular system of
active cultivation is sustained by corn alone. The
agriculture that employs and maintains millions will
leave the land, and an agriculture that employs only
thousands will take its place. Ireland will become
a pasture ground once again, as it was before, and its
agricultural population of tillage farmers and labourers
will decay and die out by degrees, or vanish and be-

come extinct at once ; even as heretofore, from the same cause in many times and countries, a population as numerous, melting away by a rapid mortality or mouldering out by slow but sure decay, have perished and passed away from the earth ; for classes of people, nor entire populations, nor nations themselves, are not fixed or immortal, any more than the individual men that compose them.

The eight thousand individuals who are owners of Ireland by divine right and the grant of God, confirmed (*by themselves*) in sundry successive acts of parliament, have a full view of these coming results I have stated, and have distinctly declared their intention of serving notice to quit on the people of Ireland. Bernal Osborne states that the small landlords are unable (*after having paid their rents*) to support themselves out of the land, and that they must be got completely rid of. The landowners have adopted the process of depopulating the island, and are pressing it forward to their own destruction, or to ours. They are declaring that they and we can no longer live together in this land. They are enforcing self-defence on us. They are, at least, forcing on us the question of submission or resistance ; and I, for one, shall give my vote for resistance.

Before I examine that question, and state what I conceive to be the true grounds, limits, and mode of resistance, I purpose making one other and last appeal to the landowners to adopt the only course that can now save a struggle.

A NATIONAL COUNCIL.

Tuesday, 25th May.

Sir,—In the leading article of last Saturday's *Nation* it is stated that the "Reproductive Committee" has changed its name, enlarged its basis, and constituted itself into what the writer would seem desirous to consider to be the nucleus of a "National Council." He seems also to attach an importance to the transaction, of which, I fear it is wholly undeserving.

The *Nation* gives no report. I have seen none elsewhere of the proceedings of the meeting at which the alleged alterations were made. I know nothing, therefore, of the name, nature, principles, or purpose, of the new association, into which the committee has resolved itself. I write, consequently, in ignorance, and on mere supposition. But I know that of necessity, it will consist effectively, if not avowedly of landowners only. Its composition and character will be determined and limited as strictly by circumstances as they could by formal rule of constitution. Originating in Dublin, without any virtual constituency through the country to empower or support, formed by its own private act, not by public action, it will never in public estimation, be anything more than an association of landowners, and it will be practical wisdom to attempt no revolt against a public decision, and to assume no other character or functions than those which general opinion will have certainly assigned to it. Should it be able to establish and extend itself, a few individuals from other classes might doubtless be induced to join it—a few mercantile and professional men, tradesmen, and tenant-farmers ; but never in sufficient number to enable it to assume the character, or exercise the functions of a National Council. Let it profess to be, what in fact, it is, an association of landed proprietors, and pretend to be nothing more. This will be its true and most effective policy. But no association of landowners, acting alone, can settle a single question of all those which are now fermenting in every house and every heart throughout the island. Be its objects what they may, the noblest or meanest, the greatest or pettiest, not one of them can be effected without the assent and aid of those who occupy the soil and inhabit the land, and who will continue to be occupiers and inhabitants in despite and defiance of open force or covert fraud, of avowed enemies or hollow friends.

If its founders, however, be honest, earnest, and capable, and should they succeed in obtaining the adhesion of any considerable number of the landed proprietors, the nascent association may be made to form one component part of a national council, of which the Commons of Ireland—tenant-farmers and trading classes—would constitute the other portion.

As the most ready and feasible mode that occurs to me of organizing such Council, I beg to present, for consideration and correction, the hasty draft of plan which is stated in the following suggestions :—

1. That the Reproductive Committee do immediately constitute itself into an association of landowners, to be composed exclusively of Irish landed proprietors.

2. That should such proposed association of land-owners become too numerous to act as a deliberate assembly, it shall appoint a managing committee of one or two hundred members, empowered and instructed to assume the office of standing, and speaking, and acting, as the accredited organ of the landed proprietors of Ireland.

3. That a tenant-league or association of tenant-farmers be formed with as little delay as possible, in each of the several counties of Ireland.

4. That every such county league of tenant-farmers shall appoint a managing committee of not less than *five* nor more than *twelve* members—the number to be fixed according to the extent and population of the county.

5. That a trade society for the revival and promotion of Irish manufacture be established in each of the thirty most populous cities and towns of the kingdom.

6. That every such trade society shall appoint a secretary, or a president and secretary, or a managing committee, of from three to eight members, according to the greater or smaller population of the town or city.

7. That these tenant-league committees, trade-committees, and trade officers, either under special powers and instructions to that effect, if allowed by the Convention Act or otherwise, through the concurrence of accidental circumstanes, or other perfectly legal and moral contrivance, shall assemble together in Dublin, to consult and determine upon such questions affecting the interests of the tenant-farmers and trading classes of Ireland, as may be brought before them, and shall further be empowered (or permitted)

to treat, confer, and enter into agreement with the
landowners' association on all these several questions.

8. That those committees be further vested with
full powers (or allowed full permission) to hold such
conference with the landed proprietors, in whatever
mode may be found most eligible and satisfactory
and on such guarantees and securities as may be
deemed sufficient.

This is a very hurried and imperfect sketch of my
ideas on the mode in which I think a National Council
might be constituted, such as the people of Ireland
would acknowledge and accept in that character.   The
primary proceeding of forming the several tenant-
leagues and trade societies is the only essential portion
of the plan.   There are many modes in which the
ulterior proceedings might be conducted without
violating the Convention Act.   If the society formed
by the " Reproductive Committee " recommend and
carry out this proceeding, or some analogous proceeding, they will have deserved well of their country,
saved and strengthened their own class, and done a
deed in history.

LETTER TO JOHN MITCHEL.

TENAKILL, ABBEYLEIX,
Tuesday, June 21st, '47.

DEAR SIR,—On receiving yours of Saturday, 19th, I determined to go at once to town without waiting for your answer to mine of Friday last, which I was aware had been posted too late for that evening's mail. I was four miles from home on my way to the coach office yesterday when a mounted servant overtook me with your letter of Sunday. On reading it I returned home : and if *your* opinions be those of the majority of the acting (I should perhaps say *talking*) members of the Council—as I take for granted they are—I scarcely know whether I can call, or consider myself any longer a member of the Confederation. Indeed I have little doubt that you go farther with me than the great majority. At least I had more dependence on you than on any other of the number—always excepting Devin Reilly. But perhaps I was wrong.

I know them and you by speeches and writing only. But men may speak and write forcibly, and yet act very feebly, and be very competent to criticise, yet utterly incompetent to construct. Ireland's greatest and last opportunity was in your hands—a revolution that would have put your own names in the blaze of the sun for ever was in your hands ; you have flung it away as the cock flung the diamond, useless to him, as the crisis was to you.

Vain to him the flash of the gem he could not polish ; vain to you were the lightnings of heaven and the meteors of earth which you could or would not kindle and guide.

Three letters of mine were published.　It was the *second*, not the *third* I said was published in *smothering silence*.

The sentence cut out of my last was " formed by and out of the same body which had produced the ' Irish Party ' formed at a private and close meeting, without public requisition, consultation, or concurrence,"—was this a misstatement of fact ?　No matter.

I never recognised the landowners as an element, or as part and portion of the people.　I recognised them as " aliens and enemies " whom I solicited to join with and *become* a part of us, and of a new Irish nation—as a " foreign garrison " whom I required to become a " national guard " before it should be too late.　*It is now too late.*　In *two months*, at least, we might appeal in vain.　Let us appeal to them, if you will, during those next two months ; but let us appeal by the only argument they can understand— the argument of *acts*—the argument of PREPARATION.

In reply to the first letter I ever received from you (March 9) I wrote to you a hurried note in which I did not precisely state my views and principles.　But I stated the main principle to Mr. D'Arcy McGee in a letter of the same date, which I requested him to hand you.　Did he do so ?　I suppose not.　At least you appear to be under mistakes as to my objects which I cannot permit you to retain.　I have nothing to do with the landlord—and—tenant question, as understood.　The question of the tenure by which the actual cultivator of the soil should hold his land is one for an Irish Parliament. My object is to repeal the Conquest—not any part or portion but the whole and entire conquest of seven hundred years— a thing much more easily done than to repeal the Union. That the absolute (allodial) ownership of the lands of Ireland is vested of right in the people of Ireland—that they, and none but they, are the first landowners and lords paramount as well as the lawmakers of this island—that all titles to land are invalid not conferred or confirmed by them—and that no man has a right to hold one foot of Irish soil otherwise than by grant of tenancy and fee from them, and under such conditions as they may annex of suit and service, faith and fealty, etc., these are my principles. To such landowners as could be brought to recognise this right of the Irish people, and to swear allegiance to this island-Queen, I would grant new titles. Those who might refuse should cease to be landowners or quit this land, and their lands be vested in the occupying tenants. The mode of argument to be employed in convincing the landlords of the truth of the principle I have stated, and of persuading them to recognise it (and Independence) is very simple. To show them we are owners *de jure*, we have only to prove we are owners *de facto*. Easily done. Our means, whether of moral agitation, military force, or moral insurrection, are impotent against the English Government, which is beyond our reach; but resistless against the English garrison who stand here, scattered and isolated, girdled round by a mighty people, whom their *leaders* alone have turned into mean slaves and sneaking beggars. Should the landlords be blind to the argument I have mentioned,

and England come to the relief and rescue of her
garrison, then of course there should be resistance
and defence, just of the kind required to drill and
discipline, as the hare-course, short and sharp, trains
and tempers and hardens the blood-hunter. The
question of time is everything. I want a prepared,
organised, and resistless revolution. *You* would
only have an unprepared, disorderly and vile jac
querie. You plead against locking the stable door
until the horse has been stolen, or is about to be
stolen. But the lock and key have yet to be forged
You won't help to forge them. But you may possibly
overtake us and help to see the door locked by others
Good. You throw away the elections too, for on no
other argument than mine will you get a frieze coat
to vote for you. Ireland was ready to strip for
battle, and none flinched but the fire-eaters. I
respectfully decline to be proposed as member of the
" Irish Council." You won't help to form *tenant-
leagues?* as a *support* or a *check.* I want that one
guarantee of the good faith of the Confederation.
Under assurance of support from them I made use
in my published letters of what must now appear as
cowardly threats, never meant to be fulfilled. I now
understand why and how Ireland is a slave. Show
this to Mr. Duffy, and to Mr. D'Arcy McGee, or to
anyone else at your own discretion. A *few months'
law* for the English garrison is all Mr. Duffy requires.
Egad !—Mr. Duffy was bred a *townsman !* A few
months—and the star of Ireland has gone down for
ever. Three-fourths of the tenant-farmers of this
county are served with ejectment notices, and this
year the bailiff follows in the track of the reaper.
The corn will be seized in the sickle.—A few months !—

Who, *what*, and *where* is Devin Reilly ? He made two speeches at the Confederation, which is all I know of him. If the man be equal to the speeches— not always the case—he ought to be the foremost man in the Confederation. As this may be possibly my last letter to you, I conclude it with some pain and regret.

Yours truly,

JAMES F. LALOR.

John Mitchel, Esq.

TENANT RIGHT MEETING IN TIPPERARY.

Mr. James F. Lalor was appointed Secretary to the meeting, and briefly explained the objects for which it was called. He said the principal object for which it was called was to establish in Tipperary the tenant right of Ulster—(cheers)—a right which declared that any man who obtained possession of land as occupying tenant should be understood as having the perpetual possession of it so long as he paid the rent—that the rent was not to be fixed by competition for the land by the landlord or agent, or be regulated by the highest bidding, but by the general standard of the country, or by common consent or by arbitration, or by some other equally fair and equable mode. So long as the rent was paid the tenant right secured the tenant against losing possession of his holding. He might sell it but could not otherwise lose it while he paid his rent. Ejectments were unknown where the tenant right was established—the landlord could not make an entry ; but if the rent fell into arrear he might sell the possession, or tenant right, in the same way as his own estate might be sold for debt. The tenant right gave the tenant as clear a right to the possession of his holding, while he met his engagement, as the landlord to the fee. The object then of the meeting was to establish the tenant right of Ulster in Tipperary, to secure the tenant perpetuity in the land and enable him to live as the tenant in Ulster lives. He would not detain the meeting longer than with these few observations, but would read to them some resolutions and allow others to speak.

LALOR'S RESOLUTIONS.

" That of natural right, on the grant of God, the soil of Ireland belongs to the people of Ireland, who have therefore a clear vested right of property in the soil to the extent of full, comfortable, and secure subsistence therefrom, which never could or can be parted with, pass, or perish ; and which no power on earth, nor any length of adverse possession can take away, annul, bar, or diminish.

" That the people of Ireland have for ages been deprived of their natural right of property in their own soil, that their right has been in practical effect utterly defeated and diverted, and that it now requires to be asserted, enforced and established.

" That the claim of the occupying tenant of the soil to a full and sufficient subsistence out of the crops they have raised, and to a sufficiency of seed for next year's crops, is prior and superior to every other claim whatsoever.

" That the subsistence of the people of Ireland is in danger, and requires to be defended, protected, and secured.

" That in defence of our rights of life and property and security of subsistence, we do hereby resolve to constitute ourselves into a public league or association, under the name of the Tipperary Tenant League."

The sixth resolution :—

" That the sole and only title that can be pleaded to any right of private property in the substance of the soil is merely and altogether conventional, and in order to be valid must be founded on common consent and agreement—be created by compact, and conferred or confirmed by the will and grant of the people, as defined or declared in the form of positive and precise laws ; and as it is thus created by the law, the law, therefore, may regulate, restrain, limit or qualify it."

The eighth resolution :—

" That the tenant right above referred to is as follows—that is to say, that any person or parties now having or holding the actual possession or occupation of any portion of the soil of this county, shall be deemed and taken to have a permanent and perpetual possession of the same, for and during so long as he shall continue to pay such rent as shall be fixed and determined by the adjudication and award of sworn arbitrators, or other fairly constituted and impartial tribunal, such adjudication and award to be made and given on such principles and in such mode as may hereafter be determined by convention and agreement between the landlord and occupier."

Other resolutions :—

" That the landlords of this country are hereby requested and called on to subscribe to and recognise the tenant right as stated in the terms of the previous resolutions, and that all lawful means be used to induce them to do so.

" That tenant farmers and people throughout the several counties of Ireland, are hereby called on to adopt the declaration of tenant right contained in the foregoing resolution, and join in covenant and agreement with us in asserting and establishing by force of public opinion the right and custom therein stated, as the standing law of tenure in Ireland.

" That provision be made for organising the league now established into divisional or parochial committees."

MR. LALOR—You see we did not come here to make speeches, but to do business. There should be a general committee of management to give effect to the resolutions, and a fund formed to be placed at the disposal of the committee. But the very first thing will be for the committee to endeavour to gain the assent of the landlords, for without their assent the object of the whole will fall to the ground."

At this point a certain Mr. William Connor claimed permission to address the meeting. He introduced himself as a worker on behalf of the farmers in other counties, and stated that he had come from Dublin to attend the meeting. In a long and spirited address he dwelt on the relative positions of landlord and tenant, arguing that the trump card held by the latter was the unfair competition, from which sprang the two great grievances—exhorbitant rents, and insecurity of tenure. This summed up the whole question, he said, and the two remedies he proposed were (1) a fair valuation of the land ; (2) a perpetuity to the tenant in his farm. He objected to Mr. Lalor's resolutions on the ground of their dubious wording.

As the resolutions had been carried, Lalor interposed with an appeal to the Chairman. Hereupon a lively argument ensued, Connor insisting on continuing his speech , Lalor denying his claim to take up the time of the meeting by lengthy harangues. Connor made use of the phrase : "The tenant right is to a great extent a delusion." To this the platform objected, and Connor was not permitted to proceed with his speech. Before he was silenced Connor made a personal attack on Lalor, saying that he and his father had oppressed "their tenantry " (though as a matter of fact they had no tenants) and refused to allow him (Connor) to organise meetings in their district. The Chairman then intervened and Connor retired;

The meeting closed, Lalor summing up as follows :— " We are determined to establish the tenant right of Ulster in this county by every means in our power— by all constitutional means—to have effect from this day forward : and the several other counties of Ireland be called on to adopt similar resolutions that a general and powerful effort be made to secure the tenant in the possession of his holding. The landlords should be requested to give their assent to the tenant right, without which the tenant would never be satisfied or the country tranquil. It will be of importance to take measures for the immediate organisation of the various divisional committees, to give effect to the resolutions passed this day. As a fund to defray expenses will also be essential, I move that a fund be raised by voluntary subscriptions."

(The motion was adopted.)

MR. LALOR'S LETTER.

To the Editor of the " IRISH FELON."

DEAR SIR,—In assenting to aid in the formation and conduct of a journal intended to fill the place and take up the mission of *The United Irishman*, I think it desirable to make a short statement of the principles and conditions, public and personal on which alone I would desire to be accepted as a partner in this undertaking. I think there is none of them to which you will object or demur, and that I may already consider them as articles of agreement. There are some of them which may possibly strike you at first as admitting question, or requiring to be qualified ; but I am convinced you will find our views to be essentially the same, although perhaps put into a different dialect and a different form of expression.

And in the first place and prior to everything else I feel bound to state that I join you on the clear understanding that I am engaging, not in a mercantile concern, nor in any private speculation or enterprise whatever, but in a political confederacy for a great public purpose. Money must not be admitted among our objects or motives ; and no money must be made by those, or any of those concerned in the conduct of this journal. You and I, and each and all of us must determine to leave this office as poor as we enter it. This condition is more important than may appear on first view ; and I believe it absolutely requisite to make, and insist on it as a principle of action. You may not, and indeed cannot be aware of all its necessity, nor of many of the motives and grounds on which I desire to have it entered as an article of agreement between ourselves, and between us and the public. In a letter intended for publication (if you see fit) I do not for the present think proper to give any full statement ; but in private I feel assured that I shall be able to satisfy your mind on this matter.

To establish an ordinary newspaper, on the common motive of vesting a capital to advantage, is doubtless quite legitimate. But to found such a journal as *The Felon*, on the views which you and I entertain, for the mere purpose, in whole or in part of making a fortune, or making a farthing, would be a felon's crime indeed, deserving no hero's doom, lamented death, or honoured exile, but death on the scaffold amid the scoff and scorn of the world. For years we have seen men in Ireland alternately trading on the government, and trading on the country, and making money by both ; and you do not imagine perhaps, to what a degree the public mind has been affected with a feeling of suspicion by the circumstance—a feeling deepened, extended, and justified by all we see or know ourselves. For indeed the craving to get money—the niggard reluctance to give money—the coward fear of losing or laying out money —is the bad or coarse point that is most apparent in the character of all ranks and classes of our people ; and I often fear it argues an utter absence of heroism from our national temperament, and of all the romantic passions, whether public or private. In other countries men marry for love ; in Ireland they marry for money. Elsewhere they serve their country for their country's thanks or their country's tears—here

they do it for their country's money. At this very
time when Ireland, to all appearance, is stripping for
her last struggle, on this side of ages, there are I am
convinced many people among the middle class who
refuse to fall into the national march, or countenance
the national movement, merely from the hope—in
most cases as vain as it is vile—of obtaining some petty
government place ; or from the fear of losing some
beggarly employment or emolument ; and I know
myself, in this county many and many a sturdy and
comfortable farmer who refuses to furnish himself
with a pike, merely and solely because it would cost
him two shillings. For ourselves—I say nothing of
others—let us aim at higher and better rewards than
mere money rewards. Better and higher rewards
has Ireland in her hands. If we succeed we shall
obtain these ; and if we do not succeed we shall de-
serve none. In cases like this the greatest crime
men can commit is the crime of failure. I am convinced it has become essential to our own fame and
our effectiveness—to the success of our cause and the
character of our country to keep clear and secure
ourselves from the suspicion that our only object
may be nothing more than a long and lucrative agitation. The Confederation pledged its members to
accept no office, or place of profit, from an English
government. That pledge was efficient, perhaps
for its own professed purpose, but not for others—
for an " agitation " has places and profits of its own
to bestow. Let them say of us whatever else they
will—let them call us felons, and treat us as such, but
let them not at least have the power to call us swindlers.
We may never be famous : let us not become infamous.
For the proprietors of this paper, let their capital be

replaced, but nothing more. For the conductors
and contributors, let their entire expenses be defrayed,
if you will, on the most liberal estimate, but nothing
more. If any surplus remains, large or little, it is
required in support and aid of our general objects,
and to that purpose I am clearly of opinion it ought
to be devoted. It is perfectly plain to me that a
newspaper cannot of itself achieve those objects, any
more than a battery can carry a camp or a fortress. A
public journal is, indeed, indispensable ; but it is
chiefly in order to cover and protect other operations,
and those operations must be paid for. For they will
not pay for themselves. A public fund is wanted—
a large one is wanted—it is wanted immediately ; and
we have no present mode of forming one, except of
throwing into it the whole surplus profits of the
Felon.

But some of us may have families—we may perish
in this enterprise—and what of them ? Leave them
to God and to Ireland ; or if you fear to trust either,
then stay at home and let others do the work.

For these, and other still more important reasons,
needless to be stated as yet, I certainly could have
wished that this journal had been established on a
subscribed capital, and the effective ownership vested
in a joint stock company of, say, eight hundred or a
thousand proprietors. What is there to hinder that
this arrangement should be made even now ? It
would contain securities and create powers which no
other could offer or pretend to. There are, indeed,
some practical difficulties in the way ; but they might
easily, I think, be overcome. Whether any such arrangement be adopted or not, I believe, however, that
I am fully warranted in desiring—and I think our own

true interest and honour concur in demanding that the
Felon office shall not be a commercial establishment,
but organised and animated as a great political association. And, for my own part, I enter it with the hope
and determination to make it an armed post, a fortress
for freedom, to be perhaps taken and retaken again,
and yet again ; but never to surrender, nor stoop
its flag, until that flag shall float above a liberated
nation.

Without agreement as to our objects we cannot
agree on the course we should follow. It is requisite
the paper should have but one object and that the
public should understand what that object is. Mine is
not to repeal the Union, nor restore Eighty-two.
This is not the year '82 ; this is the year '48. For
Repeal I never went into " Agitation " and will not
go into insurrection. On that question I refuse to
arm, or to act in any mode—and the country refuses.
O'Connell made no mistake when he pronounced it
to be not worth the price of one drop of blood ; and
for myself, I regret it was not left in the hands of
Conciliation Hall whose lawful property it was and is.
Moral force, and Repeal, the means and the purpose,
were just fitted to each other, *Arcades ambo*, balmy
Arcadians both. When the means were limited it was
only proper and necessary to limit the purpose. When
the means were enlarged, the purpose ought to have
been enlarged also. Repeal in its vulgar meaning,
I look on as utterly impracticable by any mode of
action whatever, and the constitution of '82 as absurd,
worthless, and worse than worthless. The English
government will never concede or surrender to any
species of moral force whatsoever ; and the country-
peasantry will never arm and fight for it—neither

will I. If I am to stake life and fame it must assuredly be for something better and greater, more likely to last, more likely to succeed, and better worth success. And a stronger passion, a higher purpose, a nobler and more needful enterprise is fermenting in the hearts of the people. A mightier question moves Ireland to-day than that of merely repealing the Act of Union. Not the constitution that Tone died to abolish, but the constitution that Tone died to obtain, independence, full and absolute independence, for this island, and for every man within this island. Into no movement that would leave an enemy's garrison in possession of all our lands, masters of our liberties, our lives and all our means of life and happiness—into no such movement will a single man of the greycoats enter with an armed band, whatever the town population may do. On a wider fighting field, with stronger positions and greater resources than are afforded by the paltry question of Repeal, must we close for our final struggle with England, or sink and surrender. Ireland her own—Ireland her own, and all therein, from the sod to the sky. The soil of Ireland for the people of Ireland, to have and to hold from God alone who gave it—to have and to hold to them and their heirs for ever, without suit or service, faith or fealty, rent or render, to any power under Heaven. From a worse bondage than the bondage of any foreign government, from a dominion more grievous and grinding than the dominion of England in its worst days—from the cruellest tyranny that ever yet laid its vulture clutch on the body and soul of a country, from the robber rights and robber rule that have turned us into slaves and beggars in the land that God gave us for ours.—Deliverance, oh Lord ; De-

liverance or Death—Deliverance, or this island a
desert! This is the one prayer, and terrible need,
and real passion of Ireland to-day, as it has been for
ages. Now, at last it begins to shape into defined and
desperate purpose; and into it all smaller and meaner
purposes must settle and merge. It might have been
kept in abeyance, and away from the sight of the sun—
aye, till this old native race had been finally conquered out and extinguished *sub silentio*, without
noise or notice. But once propounded and proclaimed
as a principle, not in the dusk of remote country districts, but loudly and proudly, in the tribunes of the
capital, it must now be accepted and declared, as the
first great Article of Association in the National
Covenant of organised defence and armed resistance;
as the principle to take ground, and stand and fight
upon. When a greater and more ennobling enterprise is on foot, every inferior and feebler project or
proceeding will soon be left in the hands of old women,
of dastards, impostors, swindlers, and imbeciles. All
the strength and manhood of the island—all the
courage, energies, and ambition—all the passions,
heroism, and chivalry—all the strong men, and
strong minds—all those things that make revolutions
will quickly desert it, and throw themselves into the
greater movement, throng into the larger and loftier
undertaking and flock round the banner that flies
nearest the sky. There go the young and the gallant,
the gifted, and the daring, and there too go the wise.
For wisdom knows that in national action *littleness*
is more fatal than the wildest rashness; that greatness
of object is essential to greatness of effort, strength,
and success; that a revolution ought never to take
its stand on low or narrow ground, but seize on the

broadest and highest ground it can lay hands on ; and
that a petty enterprise seldom succeeds. Had America
aimed or declared for less than independence she
would probably have failed, and been a fettered slave
to-day.

Not to repeal the Union, then, but to repeal the
Conquest—not to disturb or dismantle the empire,
but to abolish it forever—not to fall back on '82 but
act up to '48—not to resume or restore an old constitution, but to found a new nation, and raise up a
free people, and strong as well as free, and secure as
well as strong, based on a peasantry rooted like rocks
in the soil of the land—this is my object, as I hope
it is yours ; and this, you may be assured, is the
easier, as it is the nobler and more pressing enterprise.
For Repeal, all the moral means at our disposal have
been used, abused, and abandoned. All the military
means it can command will fail as utterly. Compare
the two questions. Repeal would require a national
organization ; a central representative authority,
formally convened, formally elected ; a regular army,
a regulated war of concerted action, and combined
movement. When shall we have them ? Where is
your National Council of Three Hundred ? Where is
your National Guard of Three Hundred Thousand ?
On Repeal, Ireland, of necessity, should resolve and
act *by the kingdom*, all together, linked and led ; and
if beaten in the kingdom there would be nothing to
fall back upon. She could not possibly act by parishes.
To club and arm would not be enough, or rather it
would be nothing ; and for Repeal alone Ireland will
neither club nor arm. The towns only will do so. A
Repeal-war would probably be the fight and defeat of
a single field-day ; or if protracted, it would be a mere

game of chess—and England, be assured, would beat
you in the game of chess. On the other question all
circumstances differ, as I could easily show you
But I have gone into this portion of the subject
prematurely and unawares, and here I stop—being
reluctant besides to trespass too long on the time of
her Majesty's legal and military advisers.

I would regret much to have my meaning, in any
degree, misconceived. I do not desire, by any means,
to depreciate the value and importance of Repeal,
in the valid and vigorous sense of the term, but only
in its vulgar acceptation. I do not want to make
the tenure question the sole or main topic or purpose
of the *Felon*, or to make Repeal only secondary and
subservient. I do not wish—far from it—to consider
the two questions as antagonistic or distinct. My
wish is to combine and cement the two into one ; and
so, perfect, and reinforce, and carry both. I, too,
want to bring about an alliance and " combination
of classes "—an alliance more wanted and better
worth, more feasible effective and honourable, than
any treasonable alliance with the enemy's garrison,
based on the surrender and sacrifice of the rights
and lives of the Irish people. I want to ally the town
and country. Repeal is the question of the town
population ; the land tenure question is that of the
country peasantry ; both combined, taking each in
its full extent and efficacy, form the question of
Ireland—her question for the battle-day.

The principle I state, and mean to stand upon, is
this, that the entire ownership of Ireland, moral and
material, up to the sun, and down to the centre, is
vested of right in the people of Ireland ; that they,
and none but they, are the land-owners and law-

makers of this island ; that all laws are null and void
not made by them ; and all titles to land invalid not
conferred and confirmed by them ; and that this
full right of ownership may and ought to be asserted
and enforced by any and all means which God has
put in the power of man. In other, if not plainer
words, I hold and maintain that the entire soil of a
country belongs of right to the people of that country,
and is the rightful property not of any one class, but
of the nation at large, in full effective possession, to
let to whom they will on whatever tenures, terms,
rents, services, and conditions they will ; one condition, however, being unavoidable, and essential, the
condition that the tenant shall bear full, true, and
undivided fealty, and allegiance to the nation, and the
laws of the nation whose lands he holds, and own no
allegiance whatsoever to any other prince, power, or
people, or any obligation of obedience or respect to
their will, orders, or laws. I hold further, and firmly
believe, that the enjoyment by the people of this
right, of first ownership of the soil, is essential to the
vigour and vitality of all other rights ; to their validity,
efficacy, and value ; to their secure possession and
safe exercise. For let no people deceive themselves,
or be deceived by the words, and colours, and phrases,
and forms, of a mock freedom, by constitutions, and
charters and articles, and franchises. These things
are paper and parchment, waste and worthless. Let
laws and institutions say what they will, this fact will
be stronger than all laws, and prevail against them—
the fact that those who own your land will make your
laws, and command your liberties, and your lives.
But this is tyranny and slavery—tyranny in its widest
scope, and worst shape ; slavery of body and soul from

the cradle to the coffin—slavery, with all its horrors, and with none of its physical comforts and security ; even as it is in Ireland, where the whole community is made up of tyrants. slaves, and slave-drivers. A people whose lands and lives are thus in the keeping and custody of others, instead of in their own, are not in a position of common safety. The Irish famine of '46 is example and proof. The corn crops were sufficient to feed the island. But the landlords *would* have their rents in spite of famine, and in defiance of fever. They took the whole harvest and left hunger to those who raised it. Had the people of Ireland been the landlords of Ireland, not a single human creature would have died of hunger, nor the failure of the potato been considered a matter of any consequence.

This principle, then, that the property and possession of land, as well as the powers of legislation, belong of right to people who live in the land and under the law—do you assent to it in its full integrity, and to the present necessity of enforcing it ? Your *reason* may assent, yet your *feelings* refuse and revolt—or those of others at least may do so. Mercy is for the merciful ; and you may think it pity to oust and abolish the present noble race of land-owners, who have ever been pitiful and compassionate themselves.

What ! is your sympathy for a class so great, and your sympathy for a whole people so small. For those same land-owners are now treading out the very life and existence of an entire people, and trampling down the liberties and hopes of this island for ever. It is a mere question between a people and a class—between a people of eight millions and a class of eight thousand.

They or we must quit this island. It is a people to be saved or lost—it is the island to be kept or surrendered. They have served us with a general writ of ejectment. Wherefore, I say, let them get a notice to quit at once ; or we shall oust possession under the law of nature. There are men who claim protection for them, and for all their tyrannous rights and powers, being as " one class of the Irish people." I deny the claim. They form no class of the Irish people, or of any other people. Strangers they are in this land they call theirs— strangers here and strangers everywhere, owning no country and owned by none ; rejecting Ireland, and rejected by England ; tyrants to this island, and slaves to another ; here they stand hating and hated— their hand ever against us, as ours against them, an outcast and ruffianly horde, alone in the world, and alone in its history, a class by themselves. They do not now, and never did belong to this island. Tyrants and traitors have they ever been to us and ours since first they set foot on our soil. Their crime it is and not England's that Ireland stands where she does to-day—or rather it is our own that have borne them so long. Were they a class of the Irish people the Union could be repealed without a life lost. Had they been a class of the Irish people that Union would have never been. But for them we would now be free, prosperous and happy. Until they be removed no people can ever take root, grow up and flourish here. The question between them and us must sooner or later have been brought to a deadly issue. For heaven's sake, and for Ireland's let us settle it now, and not leave it to our children to settle. Indeed it *must* be settled now—for it is plain to any ordinary sight that they or we are doomed. A cry has gone

up to heaven for the living and the dead—to save
the living, and avenge the dead.

There are, however, many landlords perhaps, and
certainly a few, not fairly chargeable with the crimes
of their order ; and you may think it hard they should
lose their lands.   But recollect, the principle I assert
would make Ireland *in fact* as she is of *right*, the
mistress and queen of all those lands ; that she, poor
lady, had ever a soft and grateful disposition ; and
that she may, if she please, in reward of allegiance,
confer new titles, or confirm the old.   Let us crown
her a queen ; and then let her do with her lands as
a queen may do.

In the case of any existing interest, of what nature
soever, I feel assured that no question but one would
need to be answered.   Does the owner of that interest
assent to swear allegiance to the people of Ireland,
and to hold in fee from the Irish nation ?   If the
assent may be assured he will suffer no loss.   No
eventual or permanent loss, I mean ; for some temporary loss he must assuredly suffer.   But such loss
would be incidental and inevitable to any armed
insurrection whatever, no matter on what principle
the right of resistance would be resorted to.   If he
refuse—then I say away with him—out of this land
with him—himself and all his robber rights, and all
the things himself and his rights have brought into our
island—blood, and tears, and famine, and the fever
that goes with famine.   Between the relative merits
and importance of the two rights, the people's right
to the land, and their right to legislation, I do not
mean or wish to institute any comparison.   I am far
indeed from desirous to put the two rights in competition, or contrast, for I consider each alike as the

natural complement of the other, necessary to its theoretical completeness, and practical efficacy. But, considering them for a moment as distinct, I do mean to assert this—that the land question contains, and the legislative question does *not* contain, the materials from which victory is manufactured ; and that, therefore, if we be truly in earnest and determined on success, it is on the former question, and not on the latter that we must take our stand, fling out our banner, and hurl down to England our gage of battle. Victory follows that banner alone, that and no other. This island is ours, and have it we will, if the leaders be true to the people, and the people be true to themselves.

The rights of property may be pleaded. No one has more respect for the real rights of property than I have ; but I do not class among them the robber's right by which the lands of this country are now held in fee for the British crown. I acknowledge no right of property in a small class which goes to abrogate the rights of a numerous people. I acknowledge no right of property in eight thousand persons, be they noble or ignoble, which takes away all rights of property, security, independence, and existence itself, from a population of eight millions, and stands in bar to all the political rights of the island, and all the social rights of its inhabitants. I acknowledge no right of property which takes away the food of millions, and gives them a famine—which denies to the peasant the right of a home, and concedes, in exchange, the right of a workhouse. I deny and challenge all such rights, howsoever founded or enforced. I challenge them, as founded only on the code of the brigand, and enforced only by the sanction of the hangman.

Against them I assert the true and indefeasible right of property—the right of our people to live in this land and possess it—to live in it in security, comfort and independence, and to live in it by their own labour, on their own land, as God and nature intended them to do. Against them I shall array, if I can, all the forces that yet remain in this island. And against them I am determined to make war—to their destruction or my own.

These are my principles and views. I shall have other opportunities to develop and defend them. I have some few other requisitions to make, but I choose to defer them for other reasons besides want of time and space. Our first business, before we can advance a step, is to fix our own footing and make good our position. That once done, this contest must if possible, be brought to a speedy close.

TO THE CONFEDERATE AND REPEAL CLUBS IN IRELAND.

(The "IRISH FELON," No. 2.)

The paper that follows was written in the last week of January, 1847—just one year and five months ago—and was forwarded to one of the leading members of the Confederation, for private circulation among the council of that body. I now address it to you just as it was written, except that I have made one or two verbal alterations, and omitted one sentence. · It might possibly be better to revise and re-write it altogether, in order to adapt it more closely to the change of date, and to present conditions. But even were I to do this there would be little to alter ; and I have reasons for preferring to publish it just as it stands.

It requires to be recollected that I was addressing a particular and picked audience, and was consequently entitled to *assume* things which it would be necessary to *prove* in addressing the general public. I assume, for example, that " moral means " alone are incompetent to achieve Repeal, because I believed that this was admitted by those I wrote for.

I see no reason to prevent me mentioning that in about a month from the date and delivery of my paper, I received a letter from John Mitchel, stating that on perusal and consideration of its contents, he had fully adopted my views, and that he meant to act on them so soon as occasion should fit and serve.

It is scarcely necessary to state that the measure I wish to have substituted for a simple Repeal of the Union was—absolute independence, with abolition of the tenures by which the lands of this country are now holden in fee for the British crown.

It will be seen that the present paper was to have been followed by a second. That second was written ; but it assumed the form of a private correspondence, addresses to several members of the Confederation, and to others—the greater portion of it to John Mitchel, between whom and myself there was from the first an *almost* perfect agreement. May his fetters weigh light, and his spirit live among us !

January 25, 1847.

In putting on paper the following ideas on the course of action which the Irish Confederation ought to take—as I am convinced it must soon and speedily fix on that course, in some more determinate shape and precise terms than it has yet thought fit to adopt— I wish it to be understood and apparent that I do not mean, and have not time to draw out anything that can purport to be a perfect and complete statement of my views on the subject, and still less to exhibit in detail the principles on which they are based, or the argument in support of them. My sole wish or intention is to *suggest*. Any attempt to *convert* or *convince* would be useless. *Individuals* are never converted ; they must convert themselves. Men are moved only in masses ; and it is easier to convert a million of men than a single man. But neither is the attempt necessary. To you, or any other of those for whom this paper in intended, the end of the clue line is enough. You will be able, *if you chose*, to follow

it out yourself. To lead on link by link would be
needless and absurd.

To any one who considers their speeches, resolutions,
and proceedings, it will, I think, appear manifest and
marked, as it does to me, that the " seceders " have
gone into organised action upon mere vague impulse
and general feeling ; with their objects undefined,
their principles unsettled, their course unmarked ;
without any determinate plan, or consequently any
fixed purpose ; for no purpose can long remain fixed,
but must be ever veering and wavering, without a
plan to guide, control, and sustain it ; and a purpose
without a plan to confine and confirm it, is no purpose
at all. Such a plan, too, is wanting as a warrant and
guarantee, to yourselves and to others that your object
is feasible, and your means adequate ; that you have
gauged your *enterprise*, and *measured* your *means* ;
and that the work you call upon us to do will not be
wasted. There are few worse things, even in the ethics
or economy of private life, than labour mis-directed ;
but what should be said of those who would, for want
of a full and éxact survey and calculation, mislead, and
exhaust the labour and means and strength of a people.
It is not principles alone, however pure, nor purposes
the highest and noblest, that ever command success ;
and few will be willing to go into a ship without
chart or compass, even though it steer its course by
the stars of heaven.

Assuming therefore, as I have a clear right to
assume, that the leading members of the Confederation, or a certain number of them, cannot long defer
coming to some agreement among themselves as to
what their objects are to be ; and that some surer
and better defined plan for attaining those objects

must be laid down and adopted than " sixty members reading-rooms, and rose-water,"—I proceed to submit the following considerations :—

1. Repeal, as *commonly understood*, taken by itself and STANDING ALONE, on its own merits and means, is an impracticable absurdity. Impracticable, because it cannot be effected except by means which would dissolve the connexion altogether, any means that can be used being either too feeble or too strong—either *inadequate* or *incompatible*. *Absurd*, because both common sense and history concur in telling us that the resulting arrangement could not possibly endure or be endured.

2. It is *impracticable*. It does not contain, nor can it command the means of possible success. It has no force to call into action on which it can rely, whether moral, military, or mixed. Its *moral* means acting in the mode admitted by the constitution, and within the limits allowed by law, are wholly incompetent ; and such as they are in Mr. O'Connell's possession, to be used, abused, or not used at all.

3. That those means are incompetent, I could easily show ; but surely it is unnecessary. The fact of incompetency will, I think, at once be recognised ; or if any one denies it, I require of him to state, in positive and precise terms, the mode of action in which those means can be made effective. The complete and ridiculous failure of every such attempt ought to be evidence sufficient on this point. The fact briefly stated is this—that a " moral agitation " ex-

hausts its whole power—its power of influencing opinion, and of producing danger, damage, and inconvenience—it exhausts this power on the country in which it takes place. It was not England, but Ireland itself that suffered evil and injury by our " glorious agitations " and " gorgeous ethic experiments." The most powerful moral agitation that could be " got up " in Ireland would not act upon *London*. If " Emancipation " be quoted, I can prove the quotation false in application to the present case.

4. But it is no less certain that those means, whether efficient or impotent, are, in full effect, the property of Mr. O'Connell. What may possibly have been the hasty and premature protest of the seceders against the Repeal question, has forced him to adopt the policy of not giving it up in *terms*. I attach no blame to the seceders for this somewhat precipitate proceeding. But the effect is that Repeal, in its constitutional shape, remains still his private property, in full, effective possession, to manage or mismanage to make much or little of, to sell or suspend, surrender or exchange as best he can. The mass of the people can neither estimate nor understand the points in dispute, nor the reasons for secession ; and can never be brought to join what could so easily be represented as an antagonistic and hostile movement. If any member of council doubts this opinion, I challenge him to *test it*.

5. The use of military means, if you had them, would be more than adequate. Those means

would do more than repeal the Union; nor
could they be limited to any such result. This
might be no objection; and I mention the fact
here, not as an objection, but for another and
different reason, which I need not state as yet.
But in truth on this question you possess no such
means nor can you command or create them;
neither, if you had them, could you employ
them with success.

6. You possess no military means. Repeal is not
an armed man, but a naked beggar. You fail
in finding the first and fundamental element
of military force—you fail in finding men. The
only martial population that Ireland possesses—
the small farmers and labourers—will never
wield a weapon in favour of Repeal. This might
be enough to say; but the full and entire fact
ought to be told, that you can never count again
on the support of the country peasantry in any
shape or degree, on the question of Repeal.
Their interest in it was never ardent; nor was
it native or spontaneous, but forced and fictitious. Such as it was, it is now extinct, and
can never be re-created. The *small farmers*,
more especially, are weary and heart-sick of
Repeal, as well as of agitation—that agitation
which has been called a bloodless one, but which
to them was not bloodless. You have with you
on Repeal—provided you can take them from
Mr. O'Connell—the *town population* of three provinces, and a portion of that of Ulster. Such
and more is the real amount of your force. This
statement may be disagreeable, and disagreeable statements are not easily believed. But

you may trust in its truth, and it requires to
be made. No error could be more fatal than a
false estimate of your force. But, be this true
or false in reference to *moral* means, you can
never make Repeal a *military* question. You
are without an army—I need not ask where
is your arsenal ?

7. But even had you those means or if you could
create them—if you had at command the whole
military power of the people and the full means
of a popular armament, I say you cannot use
them to effect on the question of Repeal. To
make it successful, your fight must be a *defensive*
one. The force of England is *entrenched* and
fortified. You must draw it out of position ;
break up its mass ; break its trained line of
march and manoeuvre, its equal step and serried
array. You cannot organize, or train, or discipline your own force to any point of efficiency.
You must therefore disorganize, and untrain,
and undiscipline that of the enemy, and not
alone must you *unsoldier*, you must *unofficer*
it also ; nullify its tactique and strategy, as
well as its discipline ; decompose the science
and system of war, and resolve them into their
first elements. You must make the hostile
army a mob, as your own will be ; force it to
act on the *offensive*, and oblige it to undertake
operations for which it was never constructed.
Nothing of all this could you do *on Repeal*. A
Repeal-war should, of necessity, be an aggressive
one on your part. You must be the attacking
party. On all the questions involved in Repeal,
England is in *occupation of the disputed points ;*

and you must assail them.   You must send your
forces against armed positions, marshal your
men for a stricken field, and full in its front,
meet England's might in unbroken mass on its
ordered march.   But further and finally, you
must get time and licence for preparing, enlisting,
organizing, drilling.   A REPEAL-war would
have to be prepared in presence of the enemy.
Need I point out to " Ulster on your flank ? "

Enough of this, and far more was needed.   I
doubt if a single man ever held the belief, *full
and firm*, that Ireland could at any time be
brought to buckle a belt and march out for
Repeal.   The tone and topics adopted by the
Nation in '43 and '44 I never attributed to anything but this—that a " glorious agitation "
affords no poetry," while insurrection *does*.   It
was the mere craving of genius for a *magnificent*
subject, instead of a *mean* one.

8. There is yet another class of means and mode
of force better founded in moral right, and more
efficient in action, than either agitation or
military insurrection.   I can find no fit and
defining name for it on the spur of the moment.
Its theory may briefly be stated as founded on
the principle of natural law—a principle beyond
dispute, denial, or doubt :—

    I That no man has any right to assume
        or claim any species of authority or juris-
        diction whatsoever over any other man,
        against the will, or without the consent of
        that other.

    II. That should he attempt to exercise such
        assumed authority over another man with-

out his consent, that other is not bound to obey.

III. And that, should he take proceedings for enforcing obedience, such proceeding may be lawfully, and ought to be, resisted by any and every means and mode of force whatsoever.

This is the rigid expression of the principle, in its first form ; and this principle, so expressed, is the nucleus round which a nation gathers and grows. Enlarged into size and expanded into shape sufficient to give ground for a people to stand on, and to fit for operation, the principle I state is this—that every distinct community or nation of men is owner of itself ; and can never of right be bound to submit to be governed by another people.

Its practical assertion forms the *third mode* of action which this country might have recourse to ; and consists :—

I. In refusal of obedience to usurped authority.

II. In maintaining and defending such refusal of obedience.

III. In resisting every attempt to exercise such usurped authority, and every proceeding adopted to enforce obedience.

IV. In taking quiet and peaceable possession of all the rights, and powers of government, and in proceeding quietly to exercise them.

V. In maintaining and defending the exercise of such rights and powers, should it be attacked.

9 I have just thought of a name for this system of means, and for want of a better, I may call

it *moral insurrection*. The difference between it and *true military* insurrection amounts to nothing more in practical effect than the difference between the *defensive* and the aggressive use of physical force—a difference, however, which is often important, whether as regards moral right or mechanical efficacy.

10. As an instrument for effecting Repeal this class of means is liable to the fatal objection stated against the preceding class. The right of moral insurrection is worthless without a military force to sustain it, and unless you be prepared and willing to use that force. On the *question of Repeal*, you have no such force. That question is too far away from the hearts of the peasantry. They do not *feel*, and scarcely understand it. They may be brought to *see its light*, but never to *feel its heat*. Other circumstances, too, render the right not available in favour of Repeal. You never could organise such an insurrection on that question. The practical assertion of the right consists of two parts :—

I. *Abolition* of British government.

II. *Formation* of a national one.

I. How would you proceed to accomplish the former ? By a general refusal to obey the entire *existing* law ? Impossible. You could not do this even *mentally* to your own satisfaction ; much less could you do it in actual fact. Or by selecting, and seizing some one particular law to take your stand on, trample down, and nullify ? What law ? The law you select for assailing must have four requisites :—First, it must form no part of the moral code ; second, it must be essential to government—a part of its substance not a mere accident—one the abrogation of which would be an abrogation of sovereignty ; third, it must be one easily disobeyed ; and fourth, difficult to enforce ; in other words, a law that would *help* to repeal itself. There is none such to serve the purpose of Repeal. In Ireland, unluckily, there is no direct and general state-tax, payment of which might be refused and resisted.

II. The second component part of the system —formation of a national government—is rendered impossible by the fact that the owners of the soil are not on your side, and are not *Irish*, but English all, in blood and feeling.

11. If those men could now at length be brought to adopt and acknowledge Ireland as their mother-country, and to give you their adhesion and support, this latter mode of moral insurrection might be put in action with success. To try the experiment of inducing them to do so seems to be the present policy and *forlorn hope* of the Confederation and the *Nation*. I am quite willing to join in trying that experiment, PROVIDED it be based and conducted on the condition that the *commons* of Ireland, as well as its *nobles*, be consulted and cared for—that the *land-owners* will consent to take the *land-holders* into council—to admit them as portion of the " Irish party "—making of that " party " **a** great national league—and finally, to frame and subscribe terms of accommodation and amnesty for the past, and articles of agreement for the future, between themselves and the

tenants of the soil—one of those articles to be security of tenure in some effective shape or other, to the present occupiers of the land.   On this basis, and on no other, would I be willing to try the experiment ; but not to make it a " life's labour."   Until the—day of—I am willing to try it—no longer.

12. But the success of that experiment is scarce to be hoped, especially now that the famine has been recognised as an " imperial calamity "—and the policy of the Confederation contains *appa-rently* no *dernier resort*—nor its proceedings any preparations for having recourse to it.   The policy I wish, and mean to press on your atten-tion, does contain such *dernier resort* ; and the course of proceeding I would fain have the Con-federation adopt contains, and comprises within it, the *preparatory* movement.

13. Repeal is not alone impracticable—as commonly understood, a simple repeal of the act of Union— it is an absurdity.   The resulting connexion and state of things could neither endure nor be endured.   Reflection tells us so—history agrees. Two independent co-equal, and sovereign legis-latures, forming one state under one crown, is an arrangement repugnant alike to common sense and experience.   Reason repudiates, and history never heard of it.   Two wheels in the same machine, of equal power, independent, unconnected, and not under control of the same prime mover, would be a better arrangement. Inanimate wheels perchance, *might* work together but under the action of human interests and passion's separate *sovereign* legislatures never

could. The examples quoted in favour of such an arrangement are beneath being urged, and beneath being answered. Between Sweden and Norway it may possibly subsist, for aught I know ; and it may continue to subsist, so long as the pulse of those countries continue to beat twenty per minute, and their blood remains at twenty degrees Fahrenheit. But when their atmosphere begins to beat up, and their blood to thaw and flow—when they shall have got a *Times* in Sweden, and a *Nation* in Norway— then will the two wheels begin to clash and crash—stop the machine, or shiver it to atoms. It subsisted between England and Ireland for *eighteen* years. But eighteen years is less in the life-time of an nation than an hour in the life of man ; and as well might you urge that two quarrelsome men, ill-affected to each other, might safely and reasonably enter into partnership for life, because they had made shift to pass an hour together, without knocking each other down. And this, too, was the very form of connection which TONE and LORD EDWARD died to repeal—as well as many others beside, whose epitaph has now at last been written, since the " better times " came ; that epitaph being short, sublime, and consoling—and encouraging too—such as Ireland awards to her dead—" *a gang of miscreants.*"

14. No mode of connexion between the kingdom could be solid, desirable, or lasting, except a *federal union*, such as that existing between New York and Pennsylvania. But a federal union must be the result of *negotiation*, and

agreement between the federating parties. I
deny the competency of the Imperial (British)
parliament to frame the act, or make the terms
of federation. But in order to negotiate, the
parties must stand on equal terms, and each be
independent of the other. *Independence*, therefore, full and entire independence, is a necessary
preli ninary to any permanent, or satisfactory
arrangement with Britain. The steps are—
independence, negotiation, and federal union.
What the terms should be I will not state,—I
dislike needless theorising.

15. Do not suppose I am insisting on useless *forms*.
My object is very different. I think every one
should familiarize his mind to the foregoing
proceeding ; for such is the proceeding, or one
analogous, which must eventually be adopted.
You will NEVER, in form of law, repeal the Act of
Union. *Never*, while the sun sits in heaven,
and the laws of nature are in action. *Never*,
before night goes down on the last day.

16. But a declaration of independence is yet far away
—at least in the distance that is measured by
events, if not in the distance that is measured
by *days*. I return to Repeal.

17. I sum up by again asserting that Repeal is
destitute of all intrinsic force, and that *standing
alone* on its own merits it does not furnish or
command the means of success.

18. Indeed so plainly apparent is the impossibility
of carrying Repeal, that its best and truest
leaders are forced to throw themselves on a
blind and helpless appeal to *futurity*. Broad
daylight is on the present, and shows too clearly

there is neither means nor hope. The future is dark; and the dark is full of shadows which fancy may shape to what forms it will; and folly may take the forms to be real. But men may keep theorising and dreaming too long— the building up or restoring an airy and ideal nationality, which time is wearing down, and wasting away, faster than they can work it up; and when they awake from their dreams they will find, I fear, that one other people has gone out of the world, as nations and races have gone ere now.

19. For a revolution is beginning which will leave Ireland *without a people*, unless it be met and conquered by a revolution which will leave it without landlords. The operation of this terrible famine will turn half the small tillage farmers—the sole strength and hope of this island—into mere labourers working for wages. The operation of the measure for repealing the corn-duties—rendered more sure and speedy by the sudden increase of demand for foreign corn—will leave landless the remainder. Heretofore, tillage land has been able to pay a higher rent than grass land. Henceforth it will be the reverse—more especially should the potato have finally failed or disappeared. The only bar that existed to the universal removal of the tillage farmer—the landlords' own personal interest in retaining him—is gone now. The result is no matter of doubt; and even if it were doubtful it ought to be provided against. Else will Ireland lose the only weapon she possesses that could conquer or cow the English government;

else, too, will she cease to have a people, for a population of pauperized labourers is not a people. I fear the English government, and *that English garrison* who say they own *our* soil, have a full view of their opportunity, and are determined to take advantage of it. We hear of nothing but plans and schemes to absorb surplus labour—the surplus labour that is in process of creation. The farmers are to pass over into the condition of labourers, and to be supported during their passage. Ireland is playing out her last game—and is she then, after all, to be checkmated, conquered, abolished? Not if her leaders and people be true and no cravens—true, not to any petty objects of personal distinction, or personal pelf—true, not to the foreign gang who call Ireland their own, and hold her lands by the robber's right—but true to their country and to themselves. One move will save checkmate. By one move alone you can meet and match—and by that same move you can checkmate England. One move alone can save the stakes now—and among those stakes are the name and fame of you and yours. Men have given to you their faith, and hearts, and hopes, for your bold bearing and bold words. Even I myself am now trusting to you and to *your* help, instead of looking round for other help and another course. Are you ready to redeem your own words, pledged in the sunshine of summer weather—are you ready to redeem them now in this day of sadness and storm? and to justify our faith when we followed your leading? Are you up to the mark and work

of this one hour, *in lieu* of the " life's labour "
you promise ?   Strip then, and bid Ireland
strip. *Now or never*, if indeed it be not too
late. Oh, for one year of the bull-dog soul of
England ! Oh, for one year of Davis now!
Whatever he may have thought *in the autumn
of* '43, his voice would have now been louder
than mine, to say what mine is too feeble to say.
He would not have lain dreaming while Ireland
was being trodden down, and her people conquered finally and for ever. For England *is now
actually winning her crowning and* DECISIVE
victory over us and ours for ages coming.

20. To prevent this result, and at the same time
achieve independence—the only form in which
Repeal can ever be carried—there is, I am convinced, but one way alone ; and that is to link
Repeal to some other question, like a railway
carriage to the engine ; some question possessing the intrinsic strength which Repeal wants ;
and strong enough to carry both itself and
Repeal together—if any such question can be
found.   And such a question there is in the land.
One ready prepared—ages have been preparing
it.   An engine ready-made—one too that will
generate its own steam without cost or care—
a self-acting engine, if once the fire be kindled ;
and the fuel to kindle—the sparks for kindling,
are everywhere.   Repeal had always to be
dragged.   This I speak of will carry itself—as
the cannon ball carries itself down the hill.

What that other question is, I may possibly
state, very briefly in another paper.

Yet if its name and general character be not
already known, I have lost my labour.

THE FIRST STEP—THE FELON CLUB.

(The " IRISH FELON " No. 2.)

The *Felon* has not been established for the mere purpose of speculating, or theorising, or teaching, but for that of acting, too. We feel the fact that it was the absence of anything like effective action that has made every Irish movement, hitherto, a ridiculous, as well as a melancholy, failure—a matter of mirth to our enemies, and of mockery to every people but ourselves.

A meeting that spreads over miles—an association that covers the island—a movement that continues through years—may each alike be just as much a mere speculator, theorist, and talker as any one individual man. And such has been the Irish Repeal movement up to this day. What was Conciliation Hall ? What was Tara ? A million of men stood there. What did they do ? Speculated, spouted, cheered, resolved, declared, petitioned, and adjourned.

We have resolved, therefore, not alone to advise others to act, but to assist them, to the utmost measure of our means, and the best of our ability ; and to adopt ourselves the most extensive and vigorous action which public support will enable us to take and maintain.

The amount of support which we could rely on as effective must be tendered us on a clear statement and full view of our principles, objects, and intended course of proceedings. All support otherwise obtained would, in effect, be obtained under false pretences ; would be altogether unsound and fictitious ; and would fail us when resorted to. We will not voluntarily deceive the public in the smallest particular, and we earnestly hope that no portion of the public will say or do aught that would tend to deceive us. We fear that public meetings in Ireland have not unfrequently applauded sentiments, and voted resolutions over night which they were utterly unprepared to act upon in the morning. But no people have a right to cheer men on to the foot of the breach, or the foot of the scaffold, and then desert them. Neither, on the other hand, ought any man leave the great mass, and general mind of the country, too far behind him. The very foremost banner should never be too far forward. In advance, but not miles nor months in advance—a stride before his regiment, a day before his people—this is a leader's place.

We hold the present existing government of this island, and all existing rights of property in our soil, to be mere usurpation and tyranny, and to be null and void as of moral effect ; and our purpose is to abolish them utterly, or lose our lives in the attempt. The right founded on conquest and affirmed by laws made by the conquerors themselves, we regard as no other than the right of the robber on a larger scale. We owe no obedience to laws enacted by another nation without our assent ; nor respect to assumed rights of property which are starving and exterminating our people. The present salvation and future security of this country require that the English government should at once be abolished, and the English garrison of landlords instantly expelled. Necessity demands it—the great necessity of self-defence. Self-defence—self-protection—it is the first law of nature, the first duty of man. We refuse all appeal to the English Parliament to abolish itself. We will not appeal against the robber to the robber's den, nor against the landlord to a Parliament of landlords. We advise the people to organize, and arm at once, in their own defence. We mean to assist them, and to set example by organizing and arming ourselves.

Such is a brief statement in outline of our principles and purposes. It leaves the principles undefended, the purposes undeveloped, all objections unanswered, all details unexplained—and details are frequently as important as principles or purposes ; but these omissions are matter of mere necessity for the present.

It remains to state our intended course of proceeding, so far as may be necessary or expedient.

We have determined to set about creating, as speedily as possible a military organization, of which the *Felon* office shall be the centre and citadel.

As our first step of proceeding we are now founding a club which, it is intended, shall consist of one, two, or more persons, from each parish throughout Ireland, who are to be in immediate connexion and correspondence with this Office.

The number of members is not intended to be limited by any positive rule. But every person is not to be admissible. Certain qualifications will be required.

As a matter of common course no man will offer himself, or be accepted as a member, unless he holds our principles, and unless he be prepared to arm, and fight in support of them when called upon.

But this will not be enough, else a common labourer unable to read or write would be eligible. Such, however is not the principle on which we are forming this Club.

But every man is eligible and acceptable who

possesses any one talent or other, or any one qualification, which would fit and enable him to be of service in any civil, military, or literary capacity, and who is willing to devote that talent or qualification to the service of his country for the next six months. It is not the *common* labour, but the *skilled* labour, we desire to engage and organize in this club.

But *zeal* ranks with us as the very chief, and is, of itself alone, a sufficient qualification.

Anyone who is qualified to form, or lead, a company, or a section of pikemen—or who is willing to head a forlorn hope—or who is able to address a public meeting, or who is competent to write a paragraph fit to appear in print—any and every such person will be gladly received as a member, and welcomed as a friend and comrade.

In one word, our object is to gather together a number of men, competent to lead in cases of necessity, and a staff of contributors competent to take the conducting of this journal, if its present conductors should be removed by death or exile. We would be very desirous to name it the Felon Club, but several local clubs have already adopted that name. We think they might resign it in our favour.

A prospectus and set of rules are in preparation, which we may publish when completed.

But without waiting for such publication, we earnestly request every man in Ireland who desires to enrol himself with us as a colleague, and comrade, and as a member of the Felon Club, will signify his wish by letter, addressed to the provisional secretary, Mr. Joseph Brennan, *Felon* office, 12 Trinity Street.

Until we have obtained at least 500 members we are resolved not to make another step in advance.   If

Ireland have not enough of confidence in us, or of heroism within herself, to furnish at least one member from each parish, we may just as well pull down our banner at once, furl it up in a corner, and fling it in the dust.

WHAT MUST BE DONE.

(The "IRISH FELON" No. 3.)

The English government is determined, it seems, to conquer and carry this office by quick assault or wearing siege. Of the hundred banners hoisted against England here, how comes it that the Felon-flag was the first to be assailed, and the second to be assailed ? Is it deemed the most dangerous, or the most defenceless—the feeblest or the most formidable ? The answer is at hand. The Castle and Conciliation, the Castle and the Confederation, the Castle and the one hundred Club-rooms, may stand together in this island ; the Castle and THE FELON office cannot stand together—one or other must give in or go down.

The hand of the English government points to this journal as the foe which it hates and fears the most. If Ireland be desirous that it shall not sink, overborne by repeated assaults, there is one sure way to support and sustain it, and but one alone. I now do what I have deferred too long—I appeal to Ireland to come to the relief of her assailed and endangered fortress ; and I claim, for sake of her own success and safety, to have the fortress manned and provided—its garrison increased, its defences strengthened. I demand the immediate formation of a joint-stock company to take Mr. Martin's place, if he should be crushed, and to continue this journal under its present or some other name.

I am proposing no new or untried idea. The *Times*, I believe, has upwards of one hundred proprietors, or had at one time ; the *Siècle* (French paper) has some thousand owners. In every undertaking, and line of business, joint-stock proprietorship is taking the place of individual ownership. What is there to put the newspaper office out of the track and operation of the same principle ? The advantages of applying it in the case of the *Felon* are obvious and easy to appreciate. An individual may be overborne or overawed, conquered, cowed or corrupted, bought, banished, or beaten down ; an individual may be feeble or foolish or fearful ; an individual may be fettered or altogether unfitted, by connections or circumstances, or inadequate means, by private views or personal jealousies ; an individual may die. A corporation or company cannot die, nor easily be conquered or committed for felony. More to show is needless. If this plan should be approved and accepted by public opinion to any efficient extent, the principles it should be carried out on are these, so far as they require to be stated now. Into details I need not enter :—

1. The company ought to be as numerous as possible —to consist of, say, from 400 to 1,200 proprietors.

2. Every one, and each of them, should be a known firm supporter of the felon principles of this journal. Absolutely requisite this.

3. The shares ought each to be very low in amount— perhaps the price of each might be fixed at £1, £2, or £2 10s. Any proprietor may, perhaps, be allowed to take as many shares as he chooses, within certain limits.

4. No share to be transferable, except to a party approved and accepted by a majority of the proprietors.

5. Some one or other of the shareholders to be selected and appointed as the registered and responsible proprietor, with a salary.

6. Four or five competent editors to be engaged, or, indeed, a greater number if possible.

7. Surplus profits of the paper, beyond a certain fixed amount (reserving or replacing proprietor's capital) to be devoted to advancing the public objects for which it will have been established.

8. Englishmen and Scotchmen to be admissible as proprietors ; and one at least of the editors to be an English Chartist of known talent and honesty. He must of course be strictly felonious, and fully prepared to aid and abet, and assist in a " premature insurrection," within the next one hundred years at farthest, as we cannot possibly afford to admit any of these doubtful characters into the establishment who first help to blow up a flame, and then help to blow it out by the free and easy use of the words " premature " " incendiary," etc.

Into further explanation or detail it is needless to go for the present.

Am I fully understood ? It is needless to say more. Am I half understood ?—it is sufficient. I can make or enable no man to *think*—I can only help him.

There may possibly be impediments or objections to this scheme which I have overlooked. If so, I desire to be made acquainted with them ; and also to be aided by suggestions for making it more efficient. These I respectfully request to have stated, as briefly as possible, by letter (and not otherwise) addressed to Mr. Joseph Brennan, FELON Office, Trinity Street. The letters must be short. A longer letter than two pages of notepaper, I never read, more especially if it be eloquently written. I hate eloquence on all subjects, particularly on *little* subjects.

Immediate written applications and proposals, absolute or conditional, addressed to Mr. Brennan, are requested from parties desirous to become shareholders in the undertaking.

Form the company I propose, and then—before they " squelch " Ireland, they must " squelch " the FELON Office. Ha! " squelch " it—by heavens—" squelch " it !* It is good. No middle course can answer that. Your knee to the ground—or death and defiance, oh Ireland !

JAMES F. LALOR.

THE FAITH OF A FELON.

(The " IRISH FELŌN " No. 3.)

When Mr. Duffy expected arrest some weeks ago he drew up his profession of principles, " The Creed of *The Nation.*" Under influence of similar feelings, and considerations, though not exactly the same nor excited by circumstances exactly alike, I hasten to put my own principles upon record. Until yesterday I did not expect to have done this for some weeks to come. The statement, or confession of faith that follows, I could have wished for time to make more correct and complete. It is ill-framed, ill-connected, and wants completeness. But even such as it stands, I do firmly believe that it carries the fortunes of Ireland; and even such as it stands, I now send it forth to its

---

* " Ireland is like a half-starved rat, that crosses the path of an elephant. What must the elephant do? Squelch it—by heavens—squelch it." *Late Letter of Thomas Carlyle.*

fate to conquer or be conquered. It may be master
of Ireland and make her a Queen ; it may lie in the
dust and perish with her people.

Here then is the confession and faith of a FELON.
Years ago I perceived that the English conquest consisted of two parts combined into one whole—the
conquest of our liberties, the conquest of our lands.

I saw clearly that the re-conquest of our liberties
would be incomplete and worthless without the
re-conquest of our lands—would not necessarily
involve or produce that of our lands and could not,
on its own means, be possibly achieved ; while the
re-conquest of our lands would involve the other,
would at least be complete in itself and adequate
to its own purposes ; and could *possibly*, if not easily,
be achieved.

The lands were owned by the conquering race, or
by traitors to the conquered race. They were occupied by the native people or by settlers who had
mingled and merged.

I selected as the *mode* of re-conquest, to refuse
payment of rent and resist process of ejectment.

In that mode I determined to effect the re-conquest
and staked on it all my hopes here and hereafter—my
hopes of an effective life and an eternal epitaph.

I was biding my time when the potato failure hurried
a crisis. The landlords and English government took
instant advantage of the famine, and the small occupiers began to quit in thousands. I saw that Ireland
was to be won at once or lost for ever. I felt her
slipping from under my feet with all her hopes, and
all my own—her lights quenching, her arm withering.

It almost seemed to me as if the Young Ireland
party, the quarrel, the secession, the Confederation,

K

had all been specially pre-ordained and produced in
order to aid me. My faith in the men who formed
the Council of that body was then unbounded. My
faith in them still is as firm as ever, though somewhat
more measured. In the paper I published last week,
and in a private correspondence that ensued with some
of its members, I proposed that they should merge
the Repeal question with a mightier project—that of
wresting this island from English rule altogether in
the only mode in which it could possibly be achieved.
I endeavoured to show them they were only keeping
up a feeble and ineffectual fire from a foolish distance
upon the English government, which stands out of
reach and beyond our power; and urged them to
wheel their batteries around and bend them on the
English garrison of landlords who stand here within
our hands, scattered, isolated, and helpless, girdled
round by the might of a people. Except two or three
of them, all refused at the time, and have persisted
in refusing until now. They wanted an alliance with
the landowners. They chose to consider them as
Irishmen, and imagined they could induce them to
hoist the green flag. They wished to preserve an
Aristocracy. They desired not a *democratic* but a
merely *national* revolution. Who imputes blame to
them for this? Whoever does so will not have
me to join him. I have no feeling but one of respect
for the motives that caused reluctance and delay.
That delay, however, I consider as matter of deep
regret. Had the Confederation, in the May or Jnue of
'47, thrown heart and mind and means and might into
the movement I pointed out, they would have made it
successful, and settled for once and forever all quarrels
and questions between us and England. I repeat

my expression of strong regret that they should not
have adopted this course, instead of persisting in a
protracted and abortive effort, at a most dangerous
conjuncture, to form an alliance of *bargain* and *barter*
with our hereditary and inveterate enemies, between
whom and the people of this island there will never
be a peace except the peace of death or of desolation.
Regrets, however are useless now.

The opinions I then stated, and which I yet stand
firm to, are these :—

1. That in order to save their own lives, the occupying tenants of the soil of Ireland ought, next autumn,
to refuse all rent and arrears of rent then due, beyond
and except the value of the overplus of harvest produce remaining in their hands after having deducted
and reserved a due and full provision for their own
subsistence during the ensuing twelve months.

2. That they ought to refuse and resist being made
beggars, landless and houseless, under the English
law of ejectment.

3. That they ought further, *on principle*, to refuse
ALL rent to the present usurping proprietors until
the people, the true proprietors (or lords paramount
in legal parlance) have in national congress or convention, decided what rents they are to pay, and *to
whom* they are to pay them.

4. And that the people on grounds of *policy* and
economy, ought to decide (as a general rule, admitting
of reservations) that those rents shall be paid *to
themselves*, the people, for public purposes, and for
behoof and benefit of them, the entire general people.

These are the principles, as clearly and fully stated
as limit of time will allow, which I advise Ireland
to adopt at once, and at once to arm for. Should the

people accept and adhere to them, the English government will then have to choose whether to surrender
the Irish landlords, or to support them with the
armed power of the empire.

If it refuse to incur the odium and expense, and to
peril the safety of England in a social war of exter-
mination, then the landlords are nobody, the people
are lords of the land, a mighty social revolution is
accomplished, and the foundations of a national revolution surely laid.   If it should on the other hand
determine to come to the rescue and relief of its garrison—elect to force their rents, and enforce their rights
by infantry, cavalry, and cannon, and attempt to lift
and carry the whole harvest of Ireland—a somewhat
heavy undertaking which might become a *hot* one
too—then I, at least, for one, am prepared to bow with
humble resignation to the dispensations of Providence.
Welcome be the will of God. We must only try to
keep our harvest, to offer a peaceful passive resistance
to barricade the island, to break up the roads, to break
down the bridges—and should need be, and occasions
offer surely we may venture to try the steel.   Other
approved modes of moral force might gradually be
added to these, as we became trained to the system :
and all combined, I imagine, and well worked, might
possibly task the strength and break the heart of the
empire.

Into artistic details, I need not, and do not choose,
to enter for the present.

It has been said to me that such a war, on the
principles I propose, would be looked on with detes-
tation by Europe.   I assert the contrary : I say such
a war would propagate itself throughout Europe.
Mark the words of this prophecy—The principle I

propound goes to the foundations of Europe, and sooner or later will cause Europe to outrise. Mankind will yet be masters of the earth. The right of the people to make the laws—this produced the first great modern earthquake, whose latest shocks even now are heaving the heart of the world. The right of the people to own the land—this will produce the next. Train your hands and your sons' hands, gentlemen of earth, for you and they will yet have to use them. I want to put Ireland foremost, in the van of the world, at the head of the nations, to set her aloft in the blaze of the sun, and to make her for ages the lode star of history. Will she take the path I point out—the path to be free and famed and feared and followed—the path that goes sunward? Or, onward to the end of time will wretched Ireland ever come limping and lagging hindmost? Events must answer that. It is a question I almost fear to look full in the face. The soul of this island seems to sink where that of another country would soar. The people sank and surrendered to the famine instead of growing savage as any other people would have done.

I am reminded that there are few persons now who trouble themselves about the " conquest "; and there may be many, I know there are some—who assent to the two first of the four principles I have stated, and are willing to accept them as the grounds of an armed movement, but who object to the last two of them. I am advised to summon the land-tenants of Ireland to stand up in battle-array for an armed struggle in defence of their rights of life and subsistence, without asserting any greater or more comprehensive right. I distinctly refuse to do so. I refuse to narrow the case and claim of the island into any such petty dimensions, or to found it on the rogue's or the beggar's plea, the plea of necessity. Not as a starving bandit, or desperate beggar who demands, to save life, what does not belong to him, do I wish Ireland to stand up, but as a decrowned Queen who claims back her own with an armed hand. I attest and urge the plea of utter and desperate necessity to fortify her claim, but not to found it. I rest it on no temporary or passing conditions but on principles that are permanent and imperishable, and universal; available to all times and to all countries, as well as to our own—I pierce through the upper stratum of occasional and shifting circumstance, to bottom and base on the rock below. I put the question in its eternal form—the form in which how often soever suppressed for a season, it can never be finally subdued, but will remain and return, outliving and outlasting the corruption and cowardice of generations. I view it as ages will view it—not through the mists of a famine but by the living lights of the firmament. You may possibly be induced to reject it in the form I propose, and accept in the other. If so you will accept the question and use it as a weapon against England, in a shape and under conditions which deprive it of half its strength. You will take and work it fettered and handcuffed not otherwise. To take it in its might, you must take it in its magnitude. I propose you should take Samson into your service. You assent but insist that his locks should be shorn. You moreover diminish and degrade down from a *national* into a mere *class* question. In the form offered it would carry independence, in the form accepted it will not even carry Repeal, in the minimum of meaning. You fling away Repeal, when you fling away the *only* mode of achieving it. For by force of arms alone can it ever be achieved ; and never on the Repeal question will you see men stand in array of battle against England.

I trouble myself as little as anyone does about the " conquest " as taken abstractedly, as an affair that took place long ages ago. But that " conquest " is still in existence with all its laws, rights, claims, relations and results. The landlord holds his lands by right and title of conquest, and uses his powers as only a conqueror may. The tenant holds under the law of conquest--*vae victis*.

Public policy must be founded on public principle ; and the question of *ethics* must be settled before the question of *economy* can be taken up or touched. If the Irish landlord's title be valid and good, no considerations of policy or economy could make a refusal to pay rent appear anything better than robbery.

What founds and forms the rights of property in land ? I have never read in the direction of that question. I have all my life been destitute of books. But from the first chapter of Blackstone's second book, the only page I ever read on the subject, I know that jurists are unanimously agreed in considering " first occupancy " to be the only true original foundation on the right of property and possession of land.

Now I am prepared to prove that " occupancy " wants every character and quality that could give it moral efficacy as a foundation of right. I am prepared to prove this when " occupancy " has first been *defined*. If no definition can be given, I am relieved from the necessity of showing any claim founded on occupancy to be weak and worthless.

Refusing, therefore, at once to accept or recognise

this feeble and fictitious title of occupancy, which was merely *invented by theorists*, and which, in actual fact was never pleaded, I proceed at once to put my own principles in order and array.

To any plain understanding the right of private property is very simple. It is the right of man to possess, enjoy, and transfer, the substance and use of whatever *he has himself* CREATED. This title is good against the world ; and it is the *sole* and *only* title by which a valid right of absolute private property can possibly vest.

But no man can plead any such title to a right of property in the substance of the soil.

The earth together with all it *spontaneously* produces is the free and common property of all mankind, of natural right, and by the grant of God ; and, all men being equal, no man, therefore, has a right to appropriate exclusively to himself any part or portion thereof, except with the *common consent* and *agreement* of all other men.

The sole original right of property which I acknowledge to be *morally* valid is this right of common consent and agreement. Every other I hold to be fabricated and fictitious, null, void and of no effect.

In the original and natural state of mankind, existing in independent families, each man must, in respect of actual fact, either *take* and *hold* (ASSUME OCCUPANCY as well as *maintain possession of*) his land by right and virtue of such consent and agreement as aforesaid, with all those who might be in a position to dispute and oppose his doing so ; or he must take and maintain possession *by force*. The fictitious right of occupancy invented by jurists to cover and account for a state of settlement otherwise unaccountable

and indefensible on moral principles—this right would
be utterly worthless, and could seldom accrue ; for
except in such a case as that of a single individual
thrown on a desert island, the *question of right* would
generally arise, and require to be settled before any
colourable " title by occupancy " could be established,
or even actual occupation be effected.   And then—
what constitutes occupancy ?   What length of possession gives " title by occupancy " ?

When independent families have united into separate
tribes, and tribes swelled into nations, the same law
obtains ; each tribe or nation has but either one or
other of two available rights to stand upon—they must
take and maintain territorial possession by consent
and agreement with all other tribes and nations ;
or they must take and hold by the *tenure of chivalry*,
in the right of their might.

In either of these two modes—that of conquest,
or that of common agreement—have the distribution
and settlement of the lands of every country been
made.   Occupancy, indeed and forsooth ! Messrs.
BLACKSTONE, TITIUS, LOCKE and Co.   Occupancy against the Goth—occupancy before the
trampling hoofs of ATTILA—occupancy to stop
HOUSTON or TAYLOR.

In every country the condition and character of
the people tell whether it was by conquest, or common
agreement, that the existing settlement and law of
landed property were established.

When it is made by agreement there will be equality
of distribution ; which equality of distribution will
remain permanent within certain limits.   For under
natural laws, landed property has rather a tendency
to divide than to accumulate.

When the independent families who form the natural population of a country compose and organise into a regular community, the imperfect compact or agreement by which each man holds his land must necessarily assume the more perfect shape of a *positive and precise grant from the people*, just as *all his other rights* must be defined and ascertained—and just as all other vague rules of agreement must organise into *laws*. That grant must necessarily assume and establish the general and common right of all the people, as joint and co-equal proprietors of all the land ; for such grant will be of itself an act of exercising and proceeding upon that right.

That grant, and all other grants must also, of necessity, without any express words, reserve the general right of the people as first proprietors and *lords paramount*, and give nothing more than a right of use and occupancy ; and it must, furthermore, recognise and reserve, in like manner, the permanent right of the people to revise, alter, and amend the mode and condition of settlement then made—and to modify or withdraw all grants made upon, or in pursuance of, that mode and condition of settlement. For no generation of living men can bind a generation that is yet unborn, or can sell or squander the rights of man ; and each generation of men has but a life interest in the world. But no generation continues the same for one hour together. Its identity is in perpetual flux. From whence it follows that, practically :—

> Any condition of settlement established, and all grants made thereupon, may, *at any time* thenceforth, be questioned, reconsidered, revised, altered, or amended.

And in order, therefore, to render the settlement a permanent one, it would be requisite to make it such as would give the majority and mass of the people a permanent interest in its maintenance.

But that object could not be accomplished by granting away the whole of the land to one man, or to *eight thousand men*, in absolute irresponsible ownership forever, without condition of payment, or any other condition whatever. This would be a settlement beyond the authority and right of any generation to make. Those deriving under it, could only be considered as holding forcible possession which any succeeding generation would have the clear right of ousting. And the people would either rise against such settlement, and trample it down—or sink under it into slaves.

Putting together and proceeding on the principles now stated, it will appear that if those principles be sound no man can legitimately claim possession or occupation of any portion of land or any right of property therein, except by grant from the people, at the will of the people, as tenant to the people, and on terms and conditions made or sanctioned by the people ; and that every right except the right so created and vested by grant from the people, is nothing more or better than the right of the robber who holds forcible possession of what does not lawfully belong to him.

The present proprietors of Ireland do not hold or claim by grant from the people, not even—except in Ulster—by any species of imperfect assent or agreement of the people. They got and keep their

lands in the robber's right—the right of conquest—
in despite, defiance, and contempt of the people.
Eight thousand men are owners of this island—claim-
ing the right of enslaving, starving, and exterminating
eight millions. We talk of asserting free government,
and of ridding ourselves of foreign domination—
while lo ! eight thousand men are lords of our lives—
of us and ours, blood and breath, happiness and
misery, body and soul. Such is the state of things
in every country where the settlement of the land
has been effected by *conquest*. In Ulster the state of
things is somewhat different, *much* to the advantage
of the people, but not so much as it ought to have
been. Ulster was not merely *conquered*, but *colonised*
—the native race being expelled, as in the United
States of America—and the settlement that prevails
was made by a sort of consent and agreement among
the conquering race.

No length of time or possession can sanction claims
acquired by robbery, or convert them into valid
rights. The people are still rightful owners, though
not in possession. " *Nullum tempus occurrit Deo—
nullum tempus occurrit populo.*"

In many countries besides this, the lands were
acquired, and long held by right of force or conquest.
But in most of them the settlement and laws of
conquest have been abrogated, amended, or modified,
to a greater or lesser extent. In some, an outrise of
the people has trampled them down—in some the
natural laws have triumphed over them—in some a
despotic monarch or minister has abolished or altered
them. In Ireland alone they remain unchanged,
unmitigated, and unmollified, in all their original
ferocity and cruelty, and the people of Ireland must

now abolish them, or be themselves abolished, and this is *now* the *more urgent* business.*

RESISTANCE.

(The " IRISH FELON," No. 4.)

Since the present contest began it is eighteen years ; and eighteen years makes a long period, and large portion in the lifetime of one generation. Since it began, youth has grown grey and manhood gone far to the grave. It must now at length, from sheer necessity, be brought to a quick determination, whether for or against us ; or it must cease altogether and forever. It can neither sustain us or be sustained any longer. And for myself I will say this, that I choose utter and eternal defeat rather than to have it last for even one year more. As hitherto con-

---

*A footnote to this article in the *Irish Felon* of July 8th states that it is incomplete. The continuation was to have been published in the following week's issue. On Saturday morning (July 8th) the " Felon " Office—12 Trinity Street—was raided by the military, and the paper seized. On the afternoon of the previous day, the Editor's room had been broken open, and all manuscripts carried off. The original MS. of Lalor's article, " The Faith of a Felon," was, in all likelihood, seized and destroyed on this occasion. Even if the unpublished portion had been in type since the printing of the paper early in the week, it could not have escaped; Lalor informs his brother, in a letter written at this time, that the " entire impression of the paper " had been seized.

The " Felon " of the following week—surreptitiously printed and sold—contains the following announcement :—

Answers to Correspondence.

" The members of the ' Felon Club ' must excuse us for not attending to their communications this week. Our office arrangements have been somewhat disturbed by the burglarious attacks of her Majesty's licensed plunderers. Some of our papers were seized —which is about the most unpleasant part of the affair. They were ' felonious ' enough, at all events; and much good may the ' felony ' do the authorities "!

ducted, it has been the most disgraceful in character and results that a nation of men was ever engaged in. It has been withering all our hearts, and wasting out our very souls—sapping all our virtues, strengthening all our vices, and making new vices of its own. It has gone far and well nigh succeeded in cowardizing a brave race and turning a nation of heroes into a nation of cravens. An age of the worst tyranny of England's worst times would be better than another year of it. Human nature itself can bear such a burthen no longer, and is sickening and sinking under it fast, longing to relieve, and if possible to redeem itself. I pronounce and record my own vote to have it end. If we be able to win, let us go in and win at once. If it be otherwise let us submit and surrender, and ask for the mercies and peace that tyranny grants to slaves.

There was force enough in this island to have brought this contest to a successful issue at any time. Not deficiency of force, but disunion, dishonesty, defect of courage, and faults of conduct, have prevented this ; for the result of thorough and determined resistance could not possibly be doubtful for a single week.

Among the many causes that have been hitherto in combination to produce failure and defeat, the one which now demands especial notice is this—that every position occupied by the people has been surrendered as soon as assailed, and every movement abandoned when met by resistance. This, in fact, has now come to be a fixed habit of action, counted and calculated on by our enemies ; if, indeed, it be not natural to us rather than formed—a matter of melancholy doubt. Irishmen, apparently, are cowed and conquered at the very point where an Englishman only begins to be throughly roused, and to fight savagely ; and more wanted, I fear, and better worth for us than a pike in every hand would be three drops of English blood in every heart—the bull-dog blood that will not sink, but boils the higher for every blow.

In the history of every successful struggle by a nation or a people, against foreign rule or domestic tyranny, one impulse and principle of action is read on every page. Wherever the force of the government was bent, there too, the people banded their force to meet it. The point of assault became the post of rally. No position was abandoned, no inch of ground was given. The attack was the signal and summons, not of surrender, but of instant, obstinate, and stern resistance. This is the road to victory— the high road ; the only road that can never lead astray ; the road from which every diverging bye-way leads to defeat ; the road that reason points out, and nature itself, and all the principles that reason acts on, and all the passions that nature owns. This is the road, and a people who can be persuaded to persist in following any other were made to be beaten, trodden down, and trampled on. Let men differ as they may about other principles, there is one that admits of no dispute, and can never be relinquished without relinquishing manhood and all its rights : the great first principle of—BLOW FOR BLOW ; blow for blow in self-defence—no matter for why or where-fore, no matter for risk or result.

And now :—

The official authorities of the English government have assailed this journal and two others—the *Nation* and *Tribune*—with the clear intent as declared by their acts, of crushing those journals, and smothering down the voice of the Irish people by naked force, violence and terror, not even disguised under forms of law, and in open violation of all those public and private rights of liberty, property and security, which they profess to defend, guard and guarantee.

Those rights we are firmly resolved on defending, and we appeal to the people of Ireland to aid us in their defence.

The Empire has declared to crush us, and we have determined to league in self-defence, and stand up to the Empire. I speak for the *Nation*, I speak for the *Tribune*, I speak for The FELON. We stand up in firm defence, and in full defiance.

We have determined to cease publication of the three journals named, and to establish another, or rather three others, the prospectus of which will be published in a few days.

But the means and resources at our command, or at the command of any small number of private individuals, would be altogether unequal to the contest we shall have to sustain ; and we therefore request the immediate formation of a company, with a paid-up capital of at least £2,000 to be subscribed in shares of £1 each for the purpose of establishing the proposed journal, and for making the requisite arrangements for its conduct and management.

Unless this be done, and until it be done, I for one of many, shall continue mute on every other matter. One thing at a time, one thing alone, until it be finished ; and here is what is first in order of importance, and necessity. If Ireland will forever, or for even one day longer, go on talking, determining, and declaring, without doing one thing practical that is proposed to her, I quit her service ; and so, too, will many others beside. We don't choose to get ourselves transported, or what is worse, get ourselves laughed at, for mere idle words that spend themselves on empty space.

The general principles on which the proposed undertaking is to be founded are stated in a paper which I published in last week's *Felon*, and out of which I now republish them. The specific rules and arrangements I have neither any reason, nor, of course, any right to undertake stating. They must be determined by consideration and agreement of the joint proprietors themselves, at their first, or some subsequent meeting.

" 1. The company ought to be as numerous as possible—to consist of, say, 400 to 1,200 proprietors.

" 2. Every one and each of them, should be a known and firm supporter of the felon principles of this journal. Absolutely requisite this.

" 3. The shares ought each be very low in amount : perhaps the price of each might be fixed at £1, £2, or £2 10s. Any proprietor may, perhaps, be allowed to take as many shares as he chooses, within certain limits.

" 4. No share to be transferable, except to a party approved and accepted by a majority of the proprietors.

" 5. Some one or other of the shareholders to be selected and appointed as a registered and responsible proprietor, with a salary.

" 6. Four or five competent editors to be engaged or indeed a greater number if possible.

" 7. Surplus profits of the paper, beyond a certain fixed sum (reserving or replacing proprietor's capital) to be devoted to advancing the public objects for which it will have been established.

" 8. Englishmen and Scotchmen to be admissable as proprietors ; and one, at least of the editors to be an English Chartist, of known talent and honesty. He must, of course, be strictly felonious, and fully prepared to aid and abet, and assist in a ' premature insurrection ' within the next hundred years at farthest."

A committee is in course of formation, for the purpose of receiving applications and proposals from parties desirous of becoming shareholders. When formed the names will be published, together with the prospectus.

CLEARING DECKS.

(The "IRISH FELON," No. 5.)

It is never the mass of a people that forms its real and efficient might. It is the men by whom that mass is moved and managed. All the great acts of history have been done by a very few men. Take half a dozen names out of any revolution upon record, and what would have been the result ?

Not Scotland but Wallace barred and baffled Edward. Not England but Cromwell struck a king from his seat. Not America, but six or eight American men, put stripes and stars on the banner of a nation. To quote examples, however, is needless. They must strike at once on every mind.

If Ireland be conquered now—or what would be

worse still, if she fails to fight—it will certainly not be the fault of the people at large—of those who form the rank and file of the nation. The failure and fault will be that of those who have assumed to take the office of commanding and conducting the march of a people for liberty, without perhaps having any commission from nature to do so, or natural right, or acquired requisite. The general population of this island are ready to find and furnish everything which can be demanded from the mass of a people—the numbers, the physical strength, the animal daring, the health, hardihood, and endurance. No population on earth of equal amount would furnish a more effective military conscription. We want only competent leaders—men of courage and capacity—men whom nature meant and made for leaders—not the praters, and pretenders, and bustling botherbys of the old agitation. Those leaders are yet to be found. Can Ireland furnish them ? It would be a sheer and absurd blasphemy against nature to doubt it. The first blow will bring them out.

But very many of our present prominent leaders must first retire or be dismissed. These men must first be got rid of utterly. They *must*. There is nothing else for it. They are stopping our way, clinging round our arms, giving us up to our enemies. Many came into this business from the mere desire of gaining a little personal distinction on safe terms and at a cheap and easy rate—of obtaining petty honours and offices—of making a small Dublin reputation—of creating a parish fame, or a tea-table fame. They will never suffer the national movement to swell beyond the petty dimensions which they are able themselves to manage and command ; and are,

therefore, a source not of strength but of weakness—
and the source of all our weakness. But for them we
could walk down the whole force of England in one
month.

In a movement of the nature of that which has been
going on for years in this country, it was impossible
to prevent the intrusion into offices of command of
that class of men who mar success instead of making
it. Indeed it was into their hands those offices have
been almost exclusively confided up to the present
hour. This can hardly be called a mistake for it was
unavoidable. The movement naturally, and of necessity, belonged to them. It was of the mock heroic
order, the machinery of which none but mean hands
would undertake or be competent to manage. The
class of men who make revolutions, and who doubtless
exist here as well as elsewhere, have been altogether
disgusted and driven away from the service of their
country by the peculiar character of that sort of
" struggle for freedom " the system of " moral agitation " which Ireland thought fit to adopt, and from
which their pride of manhood and pride of country
revolted. The staff of leaders which that system
created and has left behind it is composed of men
utterly unfit and unwilling to take charge of a military struggle, and who ought at once to be super-
seded and replaced. For two generations—may
history forget to mention them—those men have
been working to do this—the best work that ever yet
was done for tyranny—to take from the people the
terror of their name and make popular movement
a mockery. And what now are they working to do ?
To hold Ireland down hand and foot while her chains
are being locked and double-locked, and her four

noble prisoners sent fettered and handcuffed to a penal colony of England, and—hear it, O Earth, and hear it, O God ! for saying that Ireland should suffer famine no more. Oh ! worse for us than the foreign tyrant is the native traitor ; and worse than the open traitor in the enemy's ranks is the vile trickster and the base craven in our own. Away with them ! They must quit at once or be quashed. One man, and every man, of those now in the prison of Newgate is worth a host of the dastards and drivellers who are bidding you stand by and " bide your time," while your best and bravest are being transported as felons in the face of your city, in the sight of two islands, and in view of all the earth.

But how are you to know them, these menials of England in the green livery of their country ? By this shall ye know them. Any man who objects to every plan of armed resistance that is proposed, while he produces none or no better of his own. Or any man who tells you that any act of armed resistance— even if made so soon as to-morrow—even if offered by ten men only—even if offered by ten men armed only with stones—any man who tells you that such an act of resistance would be premature, imprudent, or dangerous—any and every such man should at once be spurned and spat at. For, remark you this and recollect it, that *somewhere, somehow*, and by *somebody*, a *beginning must* be made ; and that the *first* act of resistance is always, and must be ever premature, imprudent, and dangerous. Lexington was premature, Bunker's Hill was imprudent, and even Trenton was dangerous.

There are men who speak much to you of prudence and caution, and very little of any virtue beside. But every vice may call itself by the name of some virtue or other ; and of prudence there are many sorts. Cowardice may call itself, and readily pass for, caution, and of those who preach prudence, it behoves to enquire what kind of prudence it is they speak of, and to what class of prudent persons they belong themselves. There is a prudence the virtue of the wisest and bravest—there is a prudence the virtue of beggars and slaves.

Which class do those belong to who are prating now for prudence, and against premature insurrection ; while rejecting every proceeding and plan for preparation ?

Against the advice of those men, and all men such as they, I declare my own. In the case of Ireland now there is but one *fact* to deal with, and *one question* to be considered. The fact is this—that there are at present in occupation of this country some 40,000 armed men, in the livery and service of England ; and the question is—how best to kill and capture those 40,000 men.

If required to state my own individual opinion, and allowed to choose my own time, I certainly would take the time when the full harvest of Ireland shall be stacked in the haggards. But not infrequently *God* selects and sends his own seasons and occasions ; and oftentimes, too, an enemy is able to force the necessity of either fighting or failing. In the one case we ought not, in the other we surely cannot, attempt waiting for our harvest-home. If opportunity offers, we must dash at that opportunity—if driven to the wall, we must wheel for resistance. Wherefore, let us fight in September if we may—but sooner if we must.

Meanwhile, however, remember this—that somewhere, and somehow, and by somebody, a beginning

must be made.   Who strikes the first blow for Ireland ?
Who draws first blood for Ireland ?   Who wins a
wreath that will be green for ever ?

> *Felon* Office,
> Trinity Street,
> *Sunday Evening.*

DEAR RICHARD,*—I had your letter of Sunday last
in due course with its enclosure.   I hadn't time to
write one line until to-day.   The beginning you made
in Ballyroan is encouraging on many accounts.   The
paper you send is good—though I decidedly object to
one or two sentences—and some such thing I consider
absolutely requisite.   But until we get a press of our
own we couldn't either print or get it printed.   We
can't print within 10,000 of the number of copies we
could sell.   The only press in Dublin we can prevail
upon to work for us is a poor little *book*-press, very
different from a newspaper press, belonging to a man
named Shaw.   Until we can do *our own* work it need
hardly be expected we could undertake any other ;
and those who will not print a newspaper for us would
hardly print a placard for us either.   Martin says we
will have a press this week.   God send.   I shall try
to have your paper printed as soon as at all possible.

Have you been able to engage a smith, and to set
him to work ?   Tell me this.   The pulse of Dublin
goes according to the news from the country.   Every
club formed and every pike forged has its effect here.

I didn't publish the formation of Raheen or Ballyroan clubs as yet—because I wish to come out *strong*

---

* See Appendix 10.

with a list of ten or twelve Queen's County clubs at once. I hope you are forming one to-day in some other parish.

Could you arrange to have a parish-meeting got up by written placards, letters, messengers, etc., in some fine, good, stout parish on next Sunday—the adjoining parishes being invited to attend ? Reilly, Brennan, and I would go down with a flash and dazzle of pikes of every model. If three or four, or five parishes could be got to attend even to the number of twenty or thirty from each—that number of clubs could be formed at once. Let me know by return post. We would require to know on *Wednesday*, if possible, to make our arrangements.

I sent you the last *Felon* on Saturday. Did any copy (besides yours) reach the Queen's County ? What is thought by others—and what do you think—of the paper, and specially of my share in it ? Is there anything I ought to rectify ?

Will you become a member of the proposed Felon Club ?—and the others—such as Peter, young Conrahy, etc. No fee required, nor subscription. *Will* you write at *once*. I put these under cover to Father Dunne.

J. F. L.

Felon Office,
Friday.

DEAR RICHARD,—Reilly promised to procure me the instructions for the formation of Confederate Clubs this evening, in time for post. If he do, I shall send them under cover with this—but he is much hurried to day.

You may club and subscribe for the express purpose of procuring pikes, provided you don't avow any illegal purpose. The *Nation* was under some mistake. Such clubs abound here.

I saw Devin Reilly under great disadvantage in Maryborough. He is a *very* nice fellow in *all* respects.

Will you undertake to report progress in the formation of clubs—for publication, if you have no objection ; but at any rate for our own private information.

(Later.)

I now send the only portion of the Instructions Reilly can lay hands on in time. It is but a small portion, but you must do with it till the Sunday after next.

Have you got a *smith* ?

Address to me at the *Felon* Office, 12 Trinity Street.

10,000 copies *above* what can be supplied are ordered. None I fear can be sent to Abbeyleix, I will try to send you a copy.

J. F. L.

Felon Office,
Sunday, July 9*th.*

DEAR RICHARD,—I wrote to you on this day week pressing for an answer. Did you get my letter ? I put it under cover to Father Dunne. Did you answer it ? If you did not all I can say is this—I would be a great fool to' write to you any more.

Martin is in Newgate. So is Duffy. So are Hogan. K. O'Doherty, and Williams (*Shamrock*) of the *Tribune.* Our FELON was seized—the entire impression, on yesterday morning. We printed a second edition and sold it off clandestinely. Gentlemen, and even *ladies* were collared, pinioned, and the FELON *torn* out of their hands and out of their pockets, by the police. The *Nation* was seized last night, and the *Tribune*. Our office and editor's room were broken open on Friday. All manuscripts seized and carried off. *Your* letter and paper amongst them. I had brought them there to get the placard printed. I shall endeavour to send you four or five copies per coach, car, or train. They would be seized in the Post Office.

Could you come up here on *Saturday*? Things are coming to a close. I mean on *Friday*. I shall send you the paper per train, under cover to Dr. Fitzpatrick. Send for it.

If you got my letter of Sunday last and did not answer it, I give you up finally. Yours in haste.

J. F. L.

P.S.—*Monday.*—I have just heard that father is come to town. I am not sure whether I shall be able to send you the paper. Send to the Doctor's for it in any case.

P.S. 2.—I have heard that all our papers posted on Saturday went safe. I therefore post the last number. I may possibly send a batch of the three numbers under cover to Doctor F.—in the course of the week.

Will you write at once?

Address James F. Lalor, 4 St. Andrew Street, Dublin.

4 St. Andrew Street, Dublin,
Monday Evening, July 17th.

DEAR RICHARD,—Will you start for Dublin immediately on receipt of this—I send you half-note for £1.

Don't be asking foolish questions about " what good you can do," etc. Am I to tell you *through the Post Office*? Dillon and Devin Reilly join me in requesting you to come up at once. You are *wanted here*— that is sufficient. Get change for the half-note. If you can bring Peter, do so. Not one word of this to *anyone* else. Recollect this—if you don't come it is *cowardice* will prevent you. Bring your best dress. I won't detain you more than one day, if you can't conveniently stop longer. Come—even if father be dying.

Put your finger on your lips.

J. F. L.

APPENDICES.

I (a).

LETTER FROM JOHN MITCHEL TO JAMES FINTAN LALOR.

[This Letter was published in February, 1850, some six weeks after Lalor's death. Mitchel was then on board the *Neptune* off the Cape of Good Hope.—ED.]

Dublin : 8 Ontario Terrace, Rathmines,
4th January, 1848.

MY DEAR SIR,—For a month back I have been contemplating a letter to you, and have postponed it without any assignable reason. In fact and truth, I am ashamed to be forced to admit, that on the only question we ever differed about I was wholly wrong. Last summer the time had come for giving up the humbug of " conciliating classes " winning over landlords to nationality and the rest of it. Practically, last summer, I was unable for want of means to aid your schemes more than I did—I mean my own individual effort—but I ought to have urged the proper course upon our precious Council and Confederation, and, if needful, broken them up on that question.

There is no use now in regretting what I have done amiss hitherto ; but I will tell you what has at last brought me to the right way of thinking. The Irish Council, in which I really had some hope, and with which I worked conscientiously, trying to bring out what good I thought was in them, turned out a mere fraud and delusion. When the subject of tenant-right was broached, they shunned it like poison, and the great aggregate of the " peers and commoners," after dwindling down by degrees, as we came into the heart of the subject, at last came to the voting and division in a meeting of forty persons, amongst whom were not five landlords. I then made up my mind that all the symptoms of landlord nationality we had heard so much about were merely a screw applied to the English government. And when the coercion bill was introduced, and hailed with an atrocious howl of exultation by all the " better class," and when nationality faded instantly thereupon from all their meetings, and all their organs at the press, I perceived the old alliance was struck once more, farther than ever, and this bill to disarm the people, and enable landlords to eject and distrain in peace and safety, was merely the first fruit of a new alliance between our ancient enemies, on the basis of the *status quo*.

Then I was for saying so plainly in the *Nation*, and giving the people such advice as suited them in the circumstances—but I found that as I became more revolutionary, Duffy became more constitutional and safe, and insisted on preaching organization, education and so forth, with a view to some constitutional and parliamentary proceeding, at some future day ; and he, being Editor of the *Nation*, and this being the only occasion on which vital difference arose between us, I closed the connexion at once, and have not written a line for a month or more.

The *Nation*, I fear, has fallen into the merest old-womanly drivelling and snivelling, and the people are without a friend at the press.

In truth I fear it is but a lost people. I see nowhere

any gleam of spirit, or spark of vitality in it. It is a people that will pay to the last—pay away its all to those demands—coin its very heart's blood to pay withal. Yet it is not, I say, to be abandoned in despair. So long as any true Irishman has a tongue, or pen, hand, heart or brain, there is a duty and necessity on him, for the awakening and salvation of this country.

What are you doing or about to do ? I have been urged greatly by my own relatives within the last month to betake myself quietly to my profession——that of an attorney—in which I had, and yet might have, good prospects ; but I have chosen to put myself in the way of trying a fall with the enemy, on some ground or other. And so, as the most feasible thing for me, I am looking out for an opportunity of getting hold of some organ at the press. I was in Cork last week making enquiries about the *Southern Reporter*, which is for sale, and I think it is not improbable that it may be in my hands within a month ; but if not some other will.

I should mention that Reilly broke off all connexion with the *Nation* at the same time I did, and for the same reasons. He is to go with me and help me wherever I go ; so that I have no doubt we shall be able to gather an audience.

As for the Confederation, it seems likely soon to go smash upon the very same rock that broke up the *Nation*, and I have determined to change its milk-and-water course, or else to destroy it as a nuisance.

Father K. wrote to me some time ago that you had retired from interference with public affairs quite disheartened. I hope it is not so. The outlook before us is certainly dismal and black, but in any kind of storm or earthquake, there is hope. Anything that may awaken up the apathetic somnambulism in which the people walk. If not in " organization " then in disorganisation—if not in the dawning of solar day, then in the shooting upward of infernal fire, there may be help. It is better to reduce the island to a cinder than let it rot into an obscure quagmire, peopled with reptiles.

Pray write me a line and tell me what you think of all those matters.

Very truly yours,

JOHN MITCHEL.

1 (b.)

THE *IRISHMAN'S* COMMENT ON MITCHEL'S LETTER TO JAMES F. LALOR.

" Certain unscrupulous persons have published this private letter from Mr. Mitchel to Mr. Lalor. The part of it personal to the *Nation* admits of no reply under existing circumstances. Mr. Duffy was silent under keener provocation in '48 for the sake of the public cause ; his silence can only now be broken when Mr. Mitchel is a free man. But the document on the face of it suggests two considerations of a public character. In the first place, it is worth noting that it did not attain its primary object. Mr. Lalor never joined Mr. Mitchel in any manner after this period ; and never wrote one line in the *United Irishman* ; but distinctly declined to do either the one or the other. The reasons may be gathered from his own letter in the second number of the *Irish Felon*. Neither did it attain its secondary object. Mr. Duffy was not personally known to Mr. Lalor at this time, but he made his acquaintance a few months afterwards, and in June, '48, Mr. Lalor anxiously sought his co-operation in a journal, then projected, to be called the *Newgate Calendar*. In March, '49, while Mr. Duffy was still a prisoner in Richmond he offered him the editorship and chief control of the paper, which he had made some progress towards establishing by shares ; and in May, 1849, when Mr. Duffy was liberated, Mr. Lalor renewed his offer, tendering him the proprietorship (so far as it was compatible with the design of a joint-stock project) the editorship in chief, and the irresponsible control of the paper. From which it is not unreasonable to infer that Mr. Mitchel's letter was very fruitless in all respects.

" A second consideration it suggests, is the true cause of the split in the Irish Confederation. Many persons have been charged with creating and fomenting differences between Mr. Mitchel and Mr. Duffy which led to that event. But here in January, '48, before the famous three days' discussion, Mr. Mitchel tells Mr. Lalor that he regrets not having ' broken up ' the Confederation in the previous summer, and, in another paragraph, declared his determination to compel it to adopt his views, or ' destroy it as a nuisance.' The split came of this determination. But to destroy the Confederation as a nuisance did not prove so easy a matter. There were men there to say—the Confederation you cannot, and shall not, destroy. If you compel a struggle, not it, but *you* must give way. And so it proved. O'Brien, Meagher, Dillon, O'Gorman, McGee, and the other foremost men in the Confederation, affirmed as constitutional and safe the snivelling and drivelling policy of the *Nation*. At that time the French Revolution was still in the womb of time. Ireland's opportunity had not come, and a revolutionary policy was mere nonsense, founded on utter ignorance of the Celtic peasantry, and utter want of patient, practical genius. When the opportunity did come, the Moderates took the field to a man ; ' but it came too soon to enable the people to judge how ill and irrational the disorganising policy was, when it was first broached in the Confederation."

2 (a).
JOHN MITCHEL TO SMITH O'BRIEN.
(*Extract.*)

" I wish you would read carefully the paper signed J. F. Lalor in to-day's *Nation*. I do believe the landed proprietors, if they would, even now, or any considerable number of them, take to heart that proposal, could make fair and honourable terms for themselves, and become the most popular and powerful aristocracy on earth."   (24*th April*, 1847).

2 (b).
JOHN MITCHEL TO SMITH O'BRIEN.
(*Extract.*)

" I received your letter, enclosing those of Father Kenyon, Lalor, and Trenwith. And I need hardly repeat what I mentioned to you before, that my views of those gentlemen's doctrines entirely agree with yours, so far as the practical interference of the Confederation is concerned. And to that effect I have expressed myself in my replies to all three. As to the abstract justice of the case indeed, and the ultimate settlement of the tenure question, which should be kept steadily in view, my doctrine is nearly identical with Lalor's. And if Ireland were

M

now in *sui juris*, I should give all the help I could to any fair movement to realise and give effect to those doctrines. And in the meantime I hold it to be no more than bare honesty on my part and on the part of those who think with me, to say what we think on those points.

.   .   .   .   .   .

I also have full confidence in the principle of the Confederation, and mean to work steadily in accordance with it. The expostulations of my correspondents have not at all converted me ; on the contrary, I hope yet to convert them—at least two of them— not from their theories, but from their schemes of practically carrying them out ; and I hope to see Lalor and Fr. Kenyon (neither of whom we can afford to lose) working cordially with us yet.

(*8th Aug.*, 1847)

2 (c).

JOHN MITCHEL TO SMITH O'BRIEN.

(*Extract.*)

" Mr. Lalor, of whom I told you before, is prosecuting an agitation amongst the farmers in Tipperary, which I believe he means to extend into King's County, Queen's County and Kilkenny. He does not now go for the whole of his system ; but contemplates violent pressure on the landlords of those districts to coerce them into a fair settlement of the tenure question ; the coercion to take the form of non-payment to such landlords as hold out. The Confederation, of course, is not mixed up with this ; but several members of it (of whom I am one) have encouraged Lalor to go on, feeling that it is necessary for the tenants to apply a violent pressure from without, or else that neither individual landlords, nor the Irish Council, will do anything very effectual. . . . . .

" At the same time I must say I look to all this merely as a stimulus or spur to the Irish Council, and to the landlords generally. And there is no doubt, if they will be led or driven to frame and propose a fair, or a tolerably fair, scheme of tenant right, they will take the people out of the hands of Lalor, and of all revolutionists. But the time has nearly come when affairs must take a decisive turn, either in one way or the other. I sincerely hope it will be in the moderate direction." (*Sept.* 8*th*,1847).

MR. JOHN O'CONNELL'S LETTER.

Dublin,

19*th April*, 1848.

P. Lalor, Esq.

MY DEAR LALOR,—There are few men whose *hostility* or *neutrality* I would so much deplore as yours. If we have commented in the Association on individuals, or bodies adverse to us, it has not been in the proportion of one time *for fifty* that we collectively and individually have been assailed. Calumny has known no limits against some of us. Believing that my beloved father's principles are the only safe and practicable foundation for a popular body and popular effort, we were inevitably compelled, from time to time, to warn the people from being led away to join any other body where their safety would be endangered. The non-reading of certain letters was compelled by the fact that it is not allowable *even to discuss* sentiments and suggestions tending to a violation of law ; and of course if we did not discuss them after reading them aloud, the very fact of our so reading them without comment would be taken as an adoption of them.

At all times the conduct of a safe agitation is like leading a skittish colt through a fair ! But *now* at this moment of *madness* it is like having to deal with a wild bull ! If we yield an inch we are gone !

I don't expect that my words can carry any weight with them ; but I owed it to my deep regard and constant high esteem for you, and I owe it also to myself, to write these hurried lines in addition to Mr. Ray's regular answer to your favour.

I am, my dear Lalor, most sincerely and truly yours,

JOHN O'CONNELL.

DEFINITION OF POLITICAL ECONOMY.

The Right Rev. Dr. Hughes, Bishop of New York, the leading mind of the Catholic Church in America, delivered a lecture on the condition of Ireland in that city, on the 20th March, 1847. It is called " The Tyrant and His Famine," and has been published. We make one extract :—

" I may be told that famine is a visitation of Divine Providence. I do not admit that. I fear there is a blasphemy in charging on the Almighty the result of our own doings. The famine in Ireland has been for many years, like the cholera in India—indigenous. As long as it has been confined to a few cases in obscure and sequestered parts of the country, it may be said that the public administrators of the State are excusable, inasmuch as the facts did not come under their notice. But in the present instance it has attracted the attention of the world, and then they call

it God's famine. No, no! God's famine is known
by the general scarcity of food of which it is the consequence. There is no general scarcity. There has
been no general scarcity in Ireland either during the
present or the last year, except in one solitary species
of vegetable. The soil has produced its usual tribute
for the support of those by whom it was cultivated.
But political economy, finding Ireland too poor to buy
the products of its own labour, exported that harvest
to a better market, and left the people to die of famine
or live by alms.

"And this same political economy authorises the
provision merchant, even in the midst of the destitution, to keep his door locked and his sacks of corn
tied up, waiting for a 'better market,' while he
himself is perhaps at his desk describing the wretched-
ness of the people and the extent of their misery setting
forth, it may be for the eye of the First Lord of the
Treasury with what exemplary patience the poor
peasantry bear their sufferings—with what admirable
resignation they fall down through weakness at the
threshold of his warehouse, without having even
attempted to burst a door or break a window. Such
conduct is praised everywhere. Even her Britannic
Majesty, in her royal speech, does not disdain to dis-
approve of it ; and it is in truth deserving of universal
approbation, for the sacredness of property must be
maintained at all sacrifices, unless we would have
society dissolve itself again into its original elements.
Still—still the rights of life are dearer and higher than
the rights of property, and in a general famine like
the present there is no law of Heaven—no law of
nature, that forbids a starving man to seize on bread
wherever he can find it, even though it should be the

loaves of proposition on the altar of God's temple (Applause.)

" Let us be careful, then, not to blaspheme Providence, by calling this God's famine. The state— that great civil corporation which we call the state— is bound, so long as it has power to do so, to guard the life of its members against being sacrificed by famine from within, as much as against their being slaughtered by the enemy from without.

" But the vice inherent in our system of social and political economy is so settled that it eludes enquiry. You cannot trace it to the source. The poor man on whom the coroner holds an inquest has been murdered, but no one killed him. There is no external wound. There is no symptom of internal disease. Society guards him against all outward violence. It merely encircled him around, and in order to keep up what is called the regular current of trade, it allowed political economy, with an invisible hand, to apply the air-pump to the narrow limits within which he was confined, and exhaust the atmosphere of his physical life. Who did it? No one did it. Yet it was done."

GEORGE, HENRY.

Cf. Lalor : " A mightier question is in the land— one beside which Repeal dwarfs down into a petty parish question ; one on which Ireland may not alone try her right, but try the right of the world—on which you would be, not merely an assertor of old principles, often asserted and better asserted before her, an humble and feeble imitator and follower of other countries—but an original inventor, propounder, and propagandist in the van of the earth, and at the head of the nations."—(Letter to Charles Gavan Duffy.)

Henry George : " The harp and shamrock. . . Emblems of a country without nationality ; standard of a people down-trodden and oppressed ! The hour has come when they may lead the van of the great world-struggle. . . . The hour has come when they may stand for something far higher than local patriotism—something grander than national independence. The hour has come when they may stand forth to speak the world's hope, to lead the world's advance."

" But wherever, or by whom, the word must be spoken, the standard will be raised. No matter what the Irish leaders do, or do not do, it is too late to permanently settle the question on any basis short of the recognition of equal natural rights. And whether the Land League move forward or slink back, the agitation must spread to this side of the Atlantic. The Republic, the true republic, is not yet here. But her birth struggle must soon begin. Already, with that hope, her men's thoughts are stirring. Not a Republic of landlords and peasants ; not a republic of millionaires and tramps ; not a republic in which some are masters and some serve. But a republic of equal citizens, where competition becomes co-operation, and the interdependence of all gives true independence to each ; where moral progress goes hand in hand with intellectual progress, and material progress, and elevates and enfranchises even the poorest and weakest and lowliest." Pamphlet on The Irish Land Question. New York, March, 1881. Cf. Lalor—" Letter to the *Felon*." Page 52.

" In countries the most widely differing—under conditions the most diverse as to government, as to industries, as to tariffs, as to currency—you will find distress amongst the working classes ; but everywhere that you will thus find distress and destitution in the midst of wealth, you will find that the land is monopolised ; that instead of being treated as the common property of the whole people it is treated as the private property of individuals ; that for its use by labour, large revenues are extorted from the earnings of labour." (Progress and Poverty.—Book V.)

[It is interesting to note that besides Lalor, another Irish thinker profoundly influenced Henry George— William Thompson, of Cork county, whose " Enquiry into the Principles of the Distribution of Wealth most conductive to human happiness as applied to the newly proposed system of the Voluntary Equality of Wealth " was published in London, 1824.—ED.]

" THE FELON " PROSECUTION.

Mr. Reilly has addressed the following letters to the Under-Secretary and the Attorney-General :—

I.

Mosapher Lodge, Rathmines,
6th July, 1848.

Mr. T. Devin Reilly hereby informs the Attorney-General that he has this day sent the letter, of which the enclosed is a copy, to the Under-Secretary at the Castle.

The Attorney-General.

II.

Mr. T. Devin Reilly to the Under-Secretary.

Mosapher Lodge, Rathmines,
6th July, 1848.

Sir,—I understand that a warrant has been issued for the apprehension of Mr. Martin for the publication of an article, or articles, in the *Irish Felon* newspaper, to which I have hitherto been a contributor.

I am as yet unaware what precise articles these are; but if I am the author of them or any of them, I now hereby offer to avow the authorship, and to assume the entire responsibility which may devolve upon all connected with their publication; and to surrender myself to you, or to any other officer of the English government, whenever, or wheresoever you may appoint, on the sole and express condition that the warrant against Mr. Martin shall be withdrawn, and that no prosecution shall be instituted against him for any past publication in the *Felon* newspaper.

I owe it to Mr. Martin to state, that I write this letter without his knowledge, and I am certain when he shall know of it, entirely against his wish; but I consider myself bound in honour and justice to adopt this course.

I shall forward a copy of this note to the Attorney-General.

I have the honour, etc.,

T. Devin Reilly.

The Under-Secretary, Castle of Dublin.

LETTER FROM MR. JAMES F. LALOR TO THE UNDER-SECRETARY FOR IRELAND.

Felon Office,
Trinity Street.

Sir,—I understand that a warrant has been taken out against Mr. Martin on a charge of felony, founded on the publication of certain articles in the *Irish Felon* newspaper.

I have reason for believing that the only articles in that journal, which could be considered to afford grounds for such a charge, were none of them written by Mr. Martin, and were published in *opposition* to his *expressed opinion*.

May I take the freedom of requesting that you will have the goodness to inform me as to whether the charges against Mr. Martin will be withdrawn if the real writer should avow the authorship of those articles, and make himself legally responsible for them. If the warrant will be so withdrawn, on that condition such legal avowal will be given.

It would not, I think, be altogether just to make Mr. Martin answerable for articles which he did not write, and which were published against his wish.

Mr. Martin knows nothing of my intention to make the present communication.

I have the honour to remain,
Your obedient servant,   James F. Lalor.

LETTER FROM THE REV. NICHOLAS POWER TO PATRICK LALOR, Esq.

Nenagh, *August* 14*th.*

My Dear Sir,—Your son, Mr. James Lalor, was removed from the prison here at two o'clock on yesterday morning, and taken to Dublin in order to give evidence at the trial of Mr. Martin. I have not been able to learn whether he will be brought back here—the governor of the prison could not inform me. If Mr. Martin be allowed to escape Mr. Lalor will compromise himself, and incur whatever penalty Martin may be liable to, because he is resolved to assume the authorship of all the articles in the *Felon*. He was in very delicate health for some days before his removal. I was constantly beseeching him to walk about the prison grounds, but to no purpose— he spent most of his time in bed. As far as I could I have endeavoured to cheer the poor fellow by telling him all the news and supplying him with books. He complains bitterly of the privation he suffers by being deprived of newspapers—that I cannot remedy. Meagher, Leyne, and another were arrested yesterday at Holycross in this county. I had a letter this morning from a Parish Priest on the borders of the Atlantic in the county of Clare stating that his house was searched for O'Gorman by a large military and police force. He was not arrested though he was in the locality. We are perfectly tranquil in this part of the country, but the harvest prospects are most gloomy. The potatoes are gone in all quarters— the wheat crop is very bad, and nearly destroyed by the constant rain. What will become of our unhappy people during the approaching winter? It is shocking to contemplate the future.

Mr. Egan is in good health, and desires to be most kindly remembered to you.

With best regards to Mr. Jerome Lalor, I remain, dear Sir, Yours truly,

P. Lalor, Esq. NICHOLAS POWER, C.C.

SURRENDER OF MR. JOHN MARTIN.

(Published in the *Evening Freeman*, July 8th, 1848).

Mr. John Martin, proprietor of *The Irish Felon*, who had been keeping out of the way for some days in order not to be forced on his trial at the late commission under the " gagging act," surrendered himself this day to the authorities, the commission having been yesterday adjourned until the 8th August. At twelve o'clock he drove to the Head Police Office, and informed the presiding officer that he came to surrender himself, to answer the charge which he understood was made against him. The magistrate told him that he had no authority to take him into custody, and referred him to College Street Police Office, or to the magistrate who issued the warrant. Mr. Martin then proceeded to the office of the Commissioners of Police, in the Lower Castle Yard, the warrant having been issued by one of them, Mr. O'Ferrall, but there was no authority there either to arrest him. Ultimately, Sergeant Prender, who had the warrant, was found, and Mr. Martin proceeded with him to College Street Police Office. Intelligence of the matter having spread about, a large number of persons soon collected in the office and the neighbourhood, and there was a good deal of excitement manifested.

Mr. Tyndal was the presiding magistrate. Mr. Kemmis appeared for the prosecution, and Mr. Hickey attended on the part of Mr. Martin.

Mr. Tyndal asked Mr. Martin if he were aware of the information sworn against him ?

Mr. Martin : I am aware that informations have been sworn against me, but I don't know the nature of them.

Mr. Tyndal : We will have them read for you.

Mr. Martin : I do not know what the specific charge is. I am given to understand I am charged with felony under the new act of Parliament, but I do not know for what particular article.

Mr. Tyndal : The different articles which are the subject of the prosecution are set out in the infor mations.

Mr. Williams (the clerk) then read the portions of the informations which specified the several articles set out. The articles were as follows :—In *The Felon* of June the 24th, a letter addressed to the Editor of *The Irish Felon*, signed " James F. Lalor" ; in the publication of the 1st of July an article " The First Step— The Felon Club " and commencing with the words— " The *Felon* has not been established," and signed James F. Lalor ; in the publication of the same date of an article headed " To the Confederate and Repeal Clubs of Ireland," and commencing with the words— " The paper that follows " and ending with the words —" have lost my labour," and signed James F. Lalor ; another letter in the same publication addressed " To the Members of The Clubs, commencing with the words—" my friends," and ending thus—" prepare to reap it " and signed Joseph Brennan. In the same publication, " Song for the Future," commencing thus—" The land of ours," and ending " a free republic —The Felon."

Mr. Williams asked Mr. Martin if he should read the remainder of the informations ?

Mr. Martin : I don't think there is any more in the informations that I care about. Can I get a copy of these informations ?

Mr. Tyndal : The informations will be returned,

and, of course, a copy can be had. The informations state that it was your intention in publishing these letters, and articles, to depose her most gracious Majesty the Queen from her style, honour and royal name, and to levy war against her. It is my duty, under the circumstances, to send you for trial.

Mr. Martin : Perhaps you will allow me to mention —for I understand it is the only way I can communicate it to the public—that I have kept myself out of the way of the persons who, I understand, had a warrant against me, for the last few days, for this reason (which I have already stated in *The Felon* of this day ; but I understand that the paper has been seized and suppressed by the police in a manner which I consider public robbery). I wanted to get something like a fair trial ; and I apprehend that I could not have had anything like a fair trial, or any chance at all of such, if I were tried at the commission which was sitting last week and which closed on Friday. I have nothing more to say. I thought perhaps that the public might suppose I was afraid to meet the consequences of my own acts, which I am not.

Mr. Williams : There is another information sworn by Mr. Vernon, the registrar of newspapers at the Stamp Office, stating that you are the registered proprietor of *The Felon* newspaper ? Do you wish to have that information read ?

Mr. Martin : No, that is merely a matter of course. I understand that I am to be indicted under the Felony Act for certain writings which appeared in *The Felon*. I acknowledge that that paper is my property and that I am responsible for the writings, both legally and morally. I am now ready to go wherever the magistrate pleases.

Mr. Martin was then conveyed to Newgate, where he was visited in the course of the day by several of his friends.

We understand that in the manuscript of the letter published by Mr. Martin in *The Felon* of to-day he stated his intention of giving himself up to the authorities of this day. This passage was struck out by some of Mr. Martin's friends connected with the paper, but without the writer's knowledge. His friends, it appears, entertained a hope that they would induce him to abandon his intention.

The song included in the informations above mentioned was written by Master John Mitchel (son of " The Felon ") a lad between nine and ten years of age.

We understand it is intended to make application to one of the judges to have Mr. Martin admitted to bail."

BAGENAL, P. H. *

An active anti-Home Ruler, anti-Parnellite, and anti-Fenian, whose pen was busy between the years '70 and '80. An able pamphleteer, he argued to the satisfaction of sympathetic readers the absolute identity (!) of the Butt-Parnell policy, the Land and Labour agitation, and the Fenian movement. He was shrewd enough to trace back to James Fintan Lalor the principles inculcated by the Land League writers in America, and by Davitt and Parnell at home. In the early days of the Parliamentarian Party's activity, Bagenal's writings were circulated for electioneering purposes in England and the North.

* Author of *Parnellism and Crime, The American Irish and their Influence on Irish Politics. The Union* (1887–1889).

LALOR, RICHARD.

Richard, youngest brother of Fintan Lalor, was enrolled a member of the Irish Confederation of 7th April, 1847. He formed Confederate clubs in Raheen, Ballyroan, and other Abbeyleix villages, and sent reports of the work of the clubs to the *Felon*.

Later, he was distinguished in his county for his uncompromising Liberal principles ; and succeeded his father as Chairman of the famous " Queen's County Independent Club." During the early days of the Land League, he took a firm stand on the side of the tenants. His letter to John Bright (written prior to the Land Act of 1868) recalls in its independent tone, and phrasing, Fintan Lalor's address to the Landowners. "If you give us these things," he wrote, " it is still possible that England may have a renewed lease of this country—with the consent, and for the benefit of both parties. But if not she must still be prepared to hold this plundered and outraged country, as heretofore, at the point of the bayonet." Through the Club, he urged on Butt the expediency of the policy afterwards pursued by Biggar and Parnell. Besides Tenant Right he advocated Grand Jury Reform, and Amnesty of the Irish Political prisoners. A staunch Home Ruler, he was returned as member for Leix by a majority of nearly two thousand, at the memorable Election of 1880. He never swerved from his loyalty to Parnell, and the Parnellite policy ; and when " the Split " occurred he maintained his position at the great Leader's side. His death, in November, 1893, removed yet another true Irishman from the ranks of a Party, whose truth and sincerity were destined soon to be tried and found wanting.

NATIONAL BANKRUPTCY.*

(From *The Nation* of the 8th May, 1847.)

Ireland, in all social relations between her children, is still, and ever must be to them, an integral nationality. We Irish—no matter what thraldom may repress our political existence, no matter what foreign " law " may forbid us from giving to each other mutual aid and mutual defence—are, for good or ill, a family, a people. As a family we must live, or perish. British legislatures may incorporate our means of subsistence, but they cannot and will not incorporate, or participate in, the effects of their robbery, our pauperism and our ruin. These are ours—are Irish. Nor can they divide us into sections, making one British and another native. They cannot pale round one class of our people, and confine plague or penury to that. Pauperism can have no limits, save the natural boundaries of the land—no effects which are not equalised over the entire community. Thus the very slavery which consumes us, class by class, is a bond of union, becoming daily tightened, and strengthened into despair. And the desolation sweeping over us now is the political power which, if any can, must drive the starving province into nationhood.

One class of our people—the labouring class—has been for months entirely bankrupt. Others are flying into exile with what effects they can muster from their greatest creditor, the land which bore them. But

---

* [This article was the forerunner of that which Lalor criticises in his letter " A National Council." The above is explanatory of this noteworthy letter in which Lalor condenses so much economic insight, and forestalls the Co-operative theorists of our own day. —Ed.]

the social network binding this Irish nation to this
Irish rock is such, that a peasant cannot starve, but
a landlord is ruined—a farmer cannot emigrate, but
a merchant is made insolvent. As a people, we have
reached the verge of bankruptcy. The blight which
withered away millions of the labouring classes, un-
checked, spreading with the vigour and velocity of
contagion, has risen higher and higher in the social
scale—through shopkeepers, provincial merchants,
landlords, and metropolitan capitalists, to that class
which is the head and fountain of our monetary
system. In a word, trade in Ireland is at a standstill.
The Dublin merchant will not, in many instances,
give his wares to the country retailer save for money
paid down, and " there is no money in the country."
The Dublin banker (even the Bank of Ireland) is
necessitated to narrow more and more every day the
facilities of credit and discount.

Nor has this commercial distress reached its limit.
When, as must necessarily be the case, unless some
national power arise to protect what native trade
we have, and give a spur to native industry, all
banking credit shall have ceased—when usury will
take the place of discount, and the bill-broker of the
bank—when private loans will impoverish and not
enrich—when the existence of the struggling trader
will be merely the postponement of ruin—then, indeed,
the beggary of our provincialism shall have reached
its limit in anarchy.

A series of evils leads to this. Our monetary affairs
have been for forty-seven years in an unnatural state.
Our money market has always been in entire sub-
serviency to the London money market—at the beck
and will of every British capitalist. For forty-seven

years we have given to England in exports more than
we have received in imports, by a huge yearly tribute
of absentee rents and imperial taxes—a tribute drawn
from the industrial capital of the people.

These drains alone must have eventuated in bankruptcy. But the railway panic of last year, and its
ruinous effects on the small capitalists in every county,
the endemic impoverishment of this year, and the
consequent stagnation of all trade, save that of the
food speculator—and, lastly, the sudden deficit of
capital produced by an excessive panic of emigration,
have precipitated a crisis which time would have
silently, but inevitably, effected.

We must meet it now. Now, merchants and traders
of Ireland ! your fate and that of the starving peasant,
and the broken landlord, are one and indivisible. You
and they must lie down in ruin together, or rise up
mutually enfranchised. Possibly English legislators
may, in their merciful wisdom, tell you that insolvency
is in the natural way of trade—may bid it *laissez faire*,
and provide us with a huge new job, a bankruptcy
commission, with English beggars as commissioners,
to make of all Ireland " a whitened sepulchre." What
a " public work " it would be to whitewash a people !

The landlords are willing to negotiate loans, for
their purposes, in the London market, throwing the
repayment, by income tax, as much on the Irish
mercantile classes as on themselves. But, thank
Heaven ! that market will soon be closed against
all Irish loans, whether for transporting our people
or burying their labour. During the debate on
Monday night week, and on Friday night in the
English House of Commons, it was sufficiently evi-
denced that England is entering, too, on a season of

commercial distress, from which she may not arise without a chastening lesson. Depending totally on imported food, she has paid so largely in gold, and not manufactures, for the great imports of this year, that the Bank of England has closed discounts, in consequence of a deficit of bullion in proportion to its paper circulation. The moneyed interests of the city of London suffer under a like depression ; and when we remember our total dependence on that money market, we can guess at the extremity of our own financial distress. The manufacturing capitalists of England are now, too, in imminent peril. The labouring classes enter on a summer of idleness and stagnant trade. England then, or, as she is styled, " the Empire," will soon be unable to lend to Ireland, even under her own usurious, and, for us, destructive system. She may borrow largely, but only for her own people ; and her distress, while it cannot alleviate ours, must, by still further abstracting our produced and imported food, drag us still more quickly down into perdition.

Remaining inactive under her is then inevitable ruin. To hope for her assistance is folly. She, too, must share the sorrows she has, till now, escaped by inflicting them on us. We must look elsewhere for help.

We have, too, in ourselves what she has not—a recuperative power. Our people starve, not because there is insufficient food in Ireland, but because there is insufficient available capital. Our merchants are depressed, because the capital, which should circulate through their coffers among the people is locked up in banks, or is swept away in emigrant ships. We need only some medium of exchange, and some machinery by which we can bring the food in the country, and the mouths in the country, together—that is, the real capital and the labour, together. A power strong enough to stay forestallers in corn, and destroy the cruellest of speculations—a power national enough to demand, and obtain, a loan from the American Government, to whose citizens has gone that hoarded wealth, the loss of which makes proud England languish now—a power Irish enough to found an Irish bank, and not an English " Bank of Ireland " —a bank to foster, not cramp, native trade—to protect, not smother, native industry—to crutch, not cripple, native credit—a power like that, and none other, can save this island, and all its interests now.

Its materials are in " ourselves alone." In the ranks of the landlords, the merchants, the traders, the tenants, the artisans, are wise heads and bold hearts enough to found a National Council which would free Ireland, and preserve all her people, without firing a shot.

And the day may not be distant when England's rulers will be forced to fling off the mask, and say, as they said in '82, " Aid yourselves—we cannot aid you."

Are we prepared for this ?

THE RIGHTS OF LABOUR.*
(From the *Irish Tribune*, July 1st, 1848.)

Man was created free, and at the same time a social being ; in order to enjoy the advantages which

---

*[The authorship of this article is extremely doubtful. O'Donoghue includes it in his small edition of extracts from Lalor's Letters. The late Fredk. Ryan, in the *Irish Nation* supports the

society can give, each individual tacitly agrees to relinquish as much of his freedom as may be found incompatible with the existence of society. All men are abstractly equal, and should be so in law, but are not so in fact, for we find a wide difference between men, as well physically and morally as intellectually. Our actual happiness depends entirely upon the results of labour ; and as this labour is affected by our physical, moral, and intellectual powers its amount must vary with the individual, and consequently the happiness which he can enjoy will depend on himself if the basis of society is just.

Every man is entitled to an equal share of the land, and all other things which are the free gift of nature. These are the raw materials, by which, by his labour, he is to obtain the necessaries of life ; but this right he possesses only during his lifetime—he cannot will them to another, nor exert any influence on their disposal after his death. Every member of the community is entitled to an equal share of the property of those who die; but as such a division could with difficulty be made, society allows each individual to inherit the property of his father or other kinsman in lieu of the share to which he would be entitled of the general property.

---

view that it is Lalor's. Mr. P. S. O'Hegarty, writing in the same paper points out the un-Lalor-like style of the composition. In truth it has few of the fine qualities of Lalor's prose, and many characteristics of the essay of the 'prentice hand, as if it had come from the pen of a very young writer. The views set forth are certainly parallel with those advocated by Lalor, but so are all the principles of the brilliant young coterie of *Tribune* writers. It might be argued with equal justice that Lalor contributed the two Letters signed "A Felon" in the issues of June 17th and July 8th of that journal.—ED.]

The labour of man produces in most instances, more than he actually wants to support life ; this surplus, which he possesses in the form of tools, buildings, etc., is called capital or wealth, and in a flourishing state of society continually increases ; it is its possession which constitutes the real difference between the savage and civilised man. As one individual may be morally, physically, or intellectually superior to another, he will naturally, by the use of his labour obtain more products—that is, more capital or wealth—than the other : and as the arrangements of society allow the children to inherit the capital of the father, it must necessarily happen that great inequalities must exist in every society in relation to wealth ; that, in fact, there must be rich and poor. This arrangement of society is just, and could not be otherwise. Although some may be born poor, and therefore inheriting no accumulated labour or capital, they cannot, therefore, justly demand that a new distribution of wealth should take place— that the property of the rich should be given to them. But, on the other hand, society cannot demand from them to become machines, to work to an extent unheard of among savages, and yet deny them that comfort, and that share in progress which ought to be the sole end of civilisation. The poor man is entitled to live, in the fullest sense of the word, he is entitled to share in all the accumulated advantages of civilisation, not only as regards his physical happiness, but also his moral and intellectual cultivation. Why should he alone have no future, except that of suffer- ing ? Why should anyone dare to debar him of the enjoyment of domestic ties, these greatest incen- tives to virtue ?

The ancient civilisation of Greece permitted the same
inequalities of rich and poor as our modern civilisation
does ; but with the Greeks the intellectual and moral
man was the highest object of study.   They laboured
and accumulated capital ; but the rich among them,
instead of employing the whole of that accumulated
capital in debasing the men who made it, by subject-
ing them more and more or in ministering to their own
animal senses, sacrificed their merely personal comfort
to the public enjoyment of the nation.   Hence were
produced those masterpieces of art which we can only
admire, but not imitate.   The poor Athenian citizen
was not taught that his sole business on earth was to
labour incessantly, and that enjoyment was only for
the rich ; no, he felt that it was his right, his business
to discuss in the public places the affairs of his country,
to enjoy the pleasure of the theatre, to hear the great
truths enunciated by the philosophers, to attend the
games, and that it was his duty as it is in all free
states, to defend his country as a soldier.

During the Middle Ages the peasants were the
serfs of nobility ; but although the conditions of their
tenure was hard, although frequently robbed of all
the fruits of their labours, they had a real interest
in the land—an interest which in some countries they
were able to transmit to their children.   They were
poor, but not destitute, no pauper class.   Those who
did not possess land were the servants of the lords,
and as such were always sure of obtaining the first
necessaries of life.   The burgher class of the towns was
a manly race, which pursued its peaceful occupations
within the walled towns, and when necessary, defended their rights and properties by the sword against
the nobility which surrounded them, whose trade then

as now, was plundering the industrious classes. Each trade formed a guild, itself under the protection of a patron saint. The guild regulated the conditions of apprenticeship, and prevented the trade being overstocked by taking too many apprentices. This apprenticeship was a useful custom; it required a considerable sacrifice of time, and consequently of money, and, therefore, prevented too great competition; it kept up a sympathy between the employer and the employed, as the apprentice in most cases resided with the master. The apprentice's hours of labour were also limited, and thus he had ample means to improve and amuse himself. When the apprentice became a journeyman, and received wages, he did not immediately marry, but went to other towns, and worked there for some time, and thus increased his knowledge and experience; and when he accumulated sufficient capital he became a master, and settled in the place best suited to his business, took apprentices and employed journeymen, and then only did he marry. The masters in those days were only small capitalists, as each man endeavoured to be one; but they were sure of independence, for they did not believe that the market for their goods depended on unlimited production, and hence ruinous competition, but on the income of the country, on the fact of the people—the masses, possessing wealth. It is not the few rich in a country which consumes the products of labour—they only consume the luxuries, and these luxuries must always give but a precarious employment—it is the diffusion of wealth among the population generally which regulates the demand, and ensures the labourer from sudden and ruinous fluctuations, and this system of numerous small manufacturers produced that result.   And yet these masters must have been wealthy, numerous as they were, else they could not have raised those mighty symbols of religion which excite our admiration, or those beautiful though quaint town-halls, which grace even the smallest continental town.   Look at the cities of palaces, with their gorgeous frescoes, of republican Venice, Genoa the superb, and Florence.   Have our great capitalists anything similar to point to ?   Alas, no.   Our characteristics are prisons and workhouses.

What a contrast does not the condition of the poor in our days present to that which we have just noticed. A few individuals have gotten possession of the whole land, which they look upon as theirs, absolutely, to do with it whatever it may please them.   This, as it suits them, is allotted to cattle or to men, the latter being the worse treated, for although they consider them both as having been created by the Almighty for their sole use and benefit, yet as the value of the cattle is in the beasts themselves, they take care they are well fed and housed ;   but as the value of the men consists in the result of their labour, and as they are worth nothing when they are worked out, they can be replaced by new ones :   the landlord Thugs would therefore consider it a waste of capital to either feed, clothe or house them.   And when they grow dissatisfied with the amount of plunder which they can obtain, they cleanse the land of such offal and renew the stock.   These pariahs, or as they are denominated " surplus population," have no refuge in Ireland, save a shallow grave, uncoffined and unnamed, or the charnel-houses denominated " workhouses."   In England, however, they pass through another stage before they find this, their last resting-place ;   they become labourers in manufactories, and add to the number of those truly miserable and undenominated wretches who form a large proportion of the population of all manufacturing towns. Here a system commences, exactly similar in its effects to that of the landlord Thugs : a few men possessing, not real capital but money, or rather a still more fictitious one called credit, having taken advantage of the discoveries of science, establish large factories and employ labourers, not men only but women, and children of the tenderest age ; these they enclose in large, ill-ventilated rooms from the earliest dawn till night ; nay often robbing their weary bodies of their natural slumber. To them Nature displays her charms in vain ; no eloquence, no music, no poetry, as with the Greeks, the Venetians, the Florentines, is afforded them as a relaxation from their toil—nay their masters.

" Grudge them e'en the breeze, that once a week
    Might make them less weary and deject."

They become weak in body, depraved in morals, and the monotony of their employment dulls their intellect, and what is their reward ? To be badly fed, badly clothed, and worse housed, and be liable at any moment, from circumstances over which they have no control, to be deprived of all employment. This class resembling the Proletarii of the Roman Empire, is increasing with fearful rapidity, and will one day revenge all their wrongs on their oppressors, but will also, it is to be feared, destroy society itself. This class may be called the *destitute*, to distinguish them from the general poor.

With the breaking down of the old society and the commencement of the present state of things, a new

science was created which had for its object the study
of the social conditions of man : and to this science
the name of political economy has been given. This
science has attracted great attention in England,
because the evils of the present social system have
been more developed there than in any other country.
It is only there and in countries blasted by her rule
that *true pauperism* exists in all its unmitigated horrors. The desire to accumulate wealth, and the state
of things produced by this desire, naturally led every
body to study a science which he was given to understand would help him to attain his end and hence whole
libraries have been written on the subject ; but what
is termed the science of political economy in England
bears the same relation to that science as the quackery
of Parr of Holloway does to the science of medicine.

We do not, however, mean to say that the English
political economists have never enunciated any
truths ; on the contrary, a good many valuable laws
have been deduced by Adam Smith and others ; but
the errors which they have promulgated far outnumber
the truths, and have done incalculable mischief. They
have materialised everything ; with them the sole
object of existence is the production of wealth, not the
advantages which its equable distribution would have
on the community. They only look to the sum total
of the wealth of a country, even where that wealth
is in the hands of a few millionaires, while the masses
are debased paupers—with them England is the most
flourishing country in the world, because from acting
on their principles it possesses in the aggregate more
wealth than most other nations ; but they forget
that one half of the population is reduced to a state of
degradation unparallelled in Europe. They make

that *the end* for which we *live*, which most other nations consider *the means* by which we may *enjoy life*.   Under their influence the arts, abstract science, or a healthy literature can with difficulty flourish.   Sismondi's answer to Ricardo, one of the most eminent of them, gives in one sentence their whole character :   " *What, is wealth then everything ! are men absolutely nothing ?*" In Ireland what is bad in their principles has been acted upon, but the good has been totally neglected. We hear constantly our flippant *ameliorators*, the turnip-headed candidates for prominent places whose knowledge of legislation has been gleaned from the leaders of a superficial press, or the stupid speeches of a class of " gentlemen " little better informed than themselves, talk about *capital* and a few other words devoid of meaning to them.   We would be fortunate if all our economists were of the same value ;   what injury could we suffer, for instance, from such thrash as the " Clarendonian talk about Repeal," etc.?   But there are others whose poison is more insidious, and who have taken the best means to diffusing it through our veins—such as one Whately* a goodly specimen of the foreign vermin we have allowed to crawl over us—of such we must beware :   already they have received a *few lessons* from another quarter, and the *Irish Tribune* will continue the tuition from time to time.

The last number of the *Felon* contains the following advertisement :—

---

* Richard Whately, then Arcl bishop of Dublin, who propagated ¤conomical heresies in the " National " schools.

On TUESDAY NEXT,

And on every future Tuesday and Thursday, will be
published,

"THE NEWGATE CALENDAR,"

successor to

"THE IRISH TRIBUNE."

Edited by

R. D. WILLIAMS and KEVIN J. O'DOHERTY,

At present Prisoners in Newgate Gaol.

Price Twopence.

I The object of this journal is to teach the Irish
people the ways and means of their deliverance, and the uses and results of freedom
when won.

II. That it may do this effectively a third of the
journal will be occupied with military information, furnished by the ablest authorities.
Under the heads of " City Fighting," " Gue-
rilla War," " Military Engineering," and
" Munitions of War," all the requisite knowledge will be carefully arranged and classified,
and the " War Department " of *The United
Irishman* and " The Practical Instructor,"
" Easy Lessons on Military Matters " of *The
Nation* reprinted entire.

III. With the same object, the Journal will be published in convenient pocket size, at the convenient pocket price of twopence, and to

facilitate its work it will be published
TWICE A WEEK;

the opinion of the editors on the Irish Revolution being that

" If 'twere done when 'tis done,
'Twere well 'twere done quickly."

IV. Several approved Felons have promised their assistance ; and the Editors have to announce that articles will appear in early numbers from C. G. Duffy, John Martin, T. D. Reilly, T. D. McGee, M. McDermott, M. Doheny, James F. Lalor, and a host of other felonious contributors.

OFFICE : 11 TRINITY STREET.